Cycling in the
South East of England

John Grimshaw CBE

Editor: Donna Wood
Designer: Phil Barfoot
Copy Editor: Helen Ridge
Proofreader: Judith Forshaw
Picture Researchers: Alice Earle (AA)
and Jonathan Bewley (Sustrans)
Image retouching and internal repro:
Sarah Montgomery and James Tims
Cartography provided by the Mapping Services
Department of AA Publishing from data provided by
Richard Sanders and Sustrans mapping team
Research and development by: Lindsey Ryle,
Melissa Henry, Julian Hunt and Peter Hall
Supplementary text: Nick Cotton
Production: Lorraine Taylor

© Crown Copyright and database rights 2012
Ordnance Survey. 100021153

Produced by AA Publishing

Published by AA Publishing (a trading name of
AA Media Limited, whose registered office is
Fanum House, Basing View, Basingstoke
RG21 4EA; registered number 06112600).

A04632

Free cycling permits are required on some British
Waterways canal towpaths. Visit www.waterscape.com
or call 0845 671 5530.

The National Cycle Network has been made possible
by the support and co-operation of hundreds of
organisations and thousands of individuals, including:
local authorities and councils, central governments
and their agencies, the National Lottery, landowners,
utility and statutory bodies, countryside and
regeneration bodies, the Landfill Communities Fund,
other voluntary organisations, charitable trusts and
foundations, the cycle trade and industry, corporate
sponsors, community organisations and Sustrans'
supporters. Sustrans would also like to extend thanks
to the thousands of volunteers who generously
contribute their time to looking after their local
sections of the Network.

We have taken all reasonable steps to ensure that
the cycle rides in this book are safe and achievable
by people with a reasonable level of fitness. However,
all outdoor activities involve a degree of risk and the
publishers accept no responsibility for any injuries
caused to readers while following these cycle rides.

The contents of this book are believed correct at the
time of printing. Nevertheless, the publishers cannot
be held responsible for any errors or omissions or for
changes in the details given in this book or for the
consequences of any reliance on the information
provided by the same. This does not affect your
statutory rights.

Printed and bound in Dubai by Oriental Press
theAA.com/shop

Sustrans
2 Cathedral Square
College Green
Bristol BS1 5DD
www.sustrans.org.uk

Sustrans is a Registered Charity in the UK:
Number 326550 (England and Wales)
SCO39263 (Scotland).

CONTENTS

Foreword by Jon Snow   4

Introduction   6

National Cycle Network facts & figures   8

Locator map   9

Cycling with children   10

Hot tips & cool tricks   12

Bike maintenance   13

THE RIDES

1 Milton Keynes & the Grand Union Canal 14

2 Phoenix Trail   18

3 The Hanson Way   22

4 Didcot, Wantage & Ridgeway   26

5 Kennet & Avon Canal   30

6 The Jubilee River   34

7 Staines to Hampton Court   38

8 Hampton Court to Putney   42

9 Tower Bridge to Woolwich   48

10 Colne Valley Trail & Ebury Way   52

11 Lee Valley   56

12 The Basingstoke Canal   62

13 Downs Link   66

14 Winchester to Alton & Basingstoke   70

15 Fordingbridge to Brockenhurst   74

16 Coast to Coast across the IoW   77

17 Langstone Harbour   82

18 Chichester Routes   86

19 South Coast Promenades   90

20 Hove to Devil's Dyke & Lewes   94

21 Chartham to Sandwich   98

22 Hever to Tonbridge   102

23 Rye to Lydd   106

24 The Cuckoo Trail   110

25 Chalk & Channel Way   114

26 Pegwell Bay to Dover   118

27 North Kent Coast   122

Next steps   126

Join Sustrans   127

Acknowledgements   128

Cycling in Britain comes of age...

Foreword by **Jon Snow,** journalist and broadcaster

Make no mistake. History is likely to judge the first decade of the 21st century as the moment when mass-participation cycling in Britain came of age.

I write this in the aftermath of the extraordinary performance of British riders in the 2009 Tour de France, and in the summer following our record haul of cycling medals at the Beijing Olympics. These are events that have caught the media and the public interest.

But they have been accompanied spoke by spoke with an eruption of mainstream cycling for both work and leisure. For Sustrans, it is the climax of more than three decades of determined work to lift cycling provision from the margins to the centre of public life.

When Sustrans' founder John Grimshaw first spoke of thousands of miles of cycle networks across the UK, many wondered who would use them. But John understood that cycling was not only a familial infection, in which mother, father and children could combine in shared activity, but that as the green revolution took hold, many jobbing cyclists like myself would also demand the right to cycle safely to work, to the shops, to school and to see friends.

"many jobbing cyclists like myself ... demand the right to cycle safely to work"

A few years ago I took part in a bike ride from Lecce, in the South of Italy, to Venice in the North, via Brindisi, Naples, Rome, Florence and Ravenna. Beyond the eternal hill climbs, what I really noticed was the place of the bicycle on the road. Drivers slowed and gave us a wide berth wherever we encountered them. It was a sensation that I had never experienced in the UK.

But at last I think this is changing and that, as in so many other European countries, bicycles and cyclists represent a predicted element of road usage. There is still a long way to go, but Sustrans has done much to make cycling safer in Britain and these rides in South East England are fine examples.

I confess I haven't completed as many as I should have, but the Jubilee River route through Eton, and Cowes to Sandown on the Isle of Wight are great examples that I have enjoyed. From time to time I have cycled from my flat in London to my weekend retreat beyond Newbury. Until this Sustrans guide came along I was daunted by the nightmare I always regarded Reading as being. This guide cuts through Reading like butter!

We have come first in the final leg of the Tour de France for the first time in history, we have won all those Olympic medals, we have vastly expanded cycling for the masses — now's the time to start enjoying it all. Here's your guide!

Cycling to work is better than it sounds!

"From time to time I have cycled from my flat in London to my weekend retreat beyond Newbury"

Now's the time to start enjoying cycling

INTRODUCTION

The South East of England is a gem of diverse landscapes, historic towns and beautiful scenery. From the River Thames winding its way through London past Putney, Tower Bridge and Canary Wharf; to Canterbury Cathedral, the seafront at Brighton, the White Cliffs of Dover – its castle and its port; and beyond to Windsor Castle and Hampton Court Palace; the South East boasts the South Downs, Britain's newest National Park, Glorious Goodwood near Chichester and the nearby jagged coastline of inlets, harbours and ferries which take bikes to Portsmouth.

Brighton Pier

This book comprises a selection of cycle rides that will enable you to access all that the South East has to offer. There are rides which might be particularly suitable for beginners and families, rides which are for the most part away from traffic, but which could be woven into shorter everyday journeys or act as the core of a longer trip or holiday.

While only one or two rides will be right near where you live, once you've tried them we hope you'll be inspired to go further afield and explore other areas of the National Cycle Network, or find your nearest route to take you on your everyday journeys to work, the shops, the library and the post office.

For the more experienced cyclist there are longer distance options. Although most rides described in this book are no longer than 15 miles/24km (about an hour and a half at a

pleasant cycling pace), the beauty of the Network is that you can always go further. A journey out and back will make a good day's cycling adventure. Use each route offered here in your own way; as the major event, or just a fragment that forms part of a day-to-day journey. Or, at the other end of the spectrum, as one section of a longer ride fashioned around, or made possible by, a certain route.

Either way you will be riding on the National Cycle Network – over 13,000 miles of which criss-cross the country, linking up and passing through hundreds of towns and cities along its way. This Network, propelled into being with donations from the public through the National Lottery in 1995, is more than it seems, as it is intended as a catalyst to raise the profile of cycling and lead to a myriad of local cycling journeys being made as a matter of course.

London's Tower Bridge

Royal Botanic Gardens, Kew

Broad Street, Alresford

The South East is the part of Britain that lies nearest to Continental Europe, where Denmark, Germany, the Netherlands and other countries all have wonderful networks of cycling routes and enjoy as much as ten times or more cycling as a consequence – with up to a quarter of all journeys made by bike. We can only envy our neighbours their way of embracing a form of travel that is so light on CO_2 and its impact on the space around us, and so beneficial to our fitness and health.

We hope that you enjoy all the great cycling that is already available in the South East. We hope that you enjoy it so much that you want to cycle again and more often. And that you may even consider joining or supporting Sustrans so that we can do much, much more to enable many more people to choose to travel in ways that benefit their health and our environment.

NATIONAL CYCLE NETWORK FACTS & FIGURES

Most of the routes featured here are part of the National Cycle Network. The aim of this book is to enable you to sample some of the highlights of the region on two wheels, but the rides in this book are really just a taster, as there are more than 13,000 miles of Network throughout the UK to explore. More than three-quarters of us live within two miles of one of the routes.

Over one million journeys a day are made on the National Cycle Network; for special trips like fun days out and holiday bike rides, but also the necessary everyday trips; taking people to school, to work, to the shops, to visit each other and to seek out green spaces. Half of these journeys are made on foot and half by bike, with urban traffic-free sections of the Network seeing the most usage.

The National Cycle Network is host to one of the UK's biggest collections of public art. Sculptures, benches, water fountains, viewing points and award-winning bridges enhance its pathways, making Sustrans one of the most prolific commissioners of public art in the UK.

The Network came into being following the award of the first-ever grant from the Lottery, through the Millennium Commission, in 1995. Funding for the Network also came from bike retailers and manufacturers through the Bike Hub, as well as local authorities and councils UK-wide, and Sustrans' many supporters. Over 2,500 volunteer Rangers give their time to Sustrans to assist in the maintenance of the National Cycle Network by adopting sections of route in communities throughout the UK. They remove glass and litter, cut back vegetation and try to ensure routes are well signed.

Developing and maintaining the National Cycle Network is just one of the ways in which Sustrans pursues its vision of a world in which people can choose to travel in ways that benefit their health and the environment.

We hope that you enjoy using this book to explore the paths and cycleways of the National Cycle Network and we would like to thank the many hundreds of organisations who have worked with Sustrans to develop the walking and cycling routes, including every local authority and council in the UK.

MAP LEGEND

Traffic Free/On Road route

Ride Start or Finish Point

National Cycle Network (Traffic Free)

National Cycle Network (On Road)

PH	AA recommended pub
	Abbey, cathedral or priory
	Abbey, cathedral or priory in ruins
	Aquarium
	Aqueduct or viaduct
	Arboretum
	Battle site
	Bird Reserve (RSPB)
	Cadw (Welsh Heritage) site
	Campsite
	Caravan site
	Caravan & campsite
	Castle
	Cave
	Country park
	English Heritage site

	Farm or animal centre
	Garden
	Hill-fort
	Historic house
	Industrial attraction
	Marina
	Monument
	Museum or gallery
	National Nature Reserve: England, Scotland, Wales
	Local nature reserve
	National Trust property
	National Trust for Scotland property
	Picnic site
	Roman remains
	Steam railway

	Theme park
	Tourist Information Centre
	Viewpoint
	Visitor or heritage centre
	World Heritage Site (UNESCO)
	Zoo or wildlife collection
	AA golf course
	Stadium
	Indoor Arena
	Tennis
	Horse racing
	Rugby Union
	Football
	Athletics
	Motorsports
	County cricket

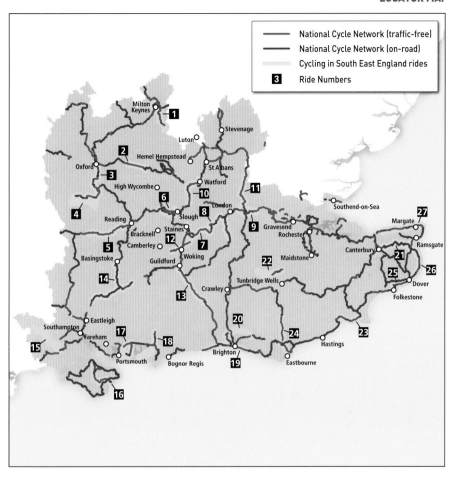

KEY TO LOCATOR MAP

1 Milton Keynes & the Grand Union Canal	**15** Fordingbridge to Brockenhurst
2 Phoenix Trail	**16** Coast to Coast across the IoW
3 The Hanson Way	**17** Langstone Harbour
4 Didcot, Wantage & Ridgeway	**18** Chichester Routes
5 Kennet & Avon Canal	**19** South Coast Promenades
6 The Jubilee River	**20** Hove to Devil's Dyke & Lewes
7 Staines to Hampton Court	**21** Chartham to Sandwich
8 Hampton Court to Putney	**22** Hever to Tonbridge
9 Tower Bridge to Woolwich	**23** Rye to Lydd
10 Colne Valley Trail & Ebury Way	**24** The Cuckoo Trail
11 Lee Valley	**25** Chalk & Channel Way
12 The Basingstoke Canal	**26** Pegwell Bay to Dover
13 Downs Link	**27** North Kent Coast
14 Winchester to Alton & Basingstoke	

CYCLING WITH CHILDREN

Kids love bikes and love to ride. Cycling helps them to grow up fit, healthy and independent, and introduces them to the wider world and the adventure it holds.

TOP TIPS FOR FAMILY BIKE RIDES:

- Take along snacks, drinks and treats to keep their energy and spirit levels up.
- Don't be too ambitious. It's much better that everyone wants to go out again, than all coming home exhausted, tearful and permanently put off cycling.
- Plan your trip around interesting stops and sights along the way. Don't make journey times any longer than children are happy to sit and play at home.
- Even on a fine day, take extra clothes and waterproofs – just in case. Check that trousers and laces can't get caught in the chain when pedalling along.
- Wrap up toddlers. When a young child is on the back of a bike, they won't be generating heat like the person doing all the pedalling!
- Be careful not to pinch their skin when putting their helmet on. It's easily done and often ends in tears. Just place your forefinger between the clip and the chin.
- Ride in a line with the children in the middle of the adults. If there's only one of you, the adult should be at the rear, keeping an eye on all the children in front. Take special care at road junctions.
- Check that children's bikes are ready to ride. Do the brakes and gears work? Is the saddle the right height? Are the tyres pumped up?
- Carry some sticking plasters and antiseptic wipes – kids are far more likely to fall off and graze arms, hands or knees.
- Take a camera to record the trip – memories are made of this.

TRANSPORTING YOUNG CHILDREN ON TWO WHEELS

It's now easier than ever for you to ride your bike with young children.

- **Child seats:** *6 months to five years (one child).* Once a baby can support its own head (usually at 6–12 months) they can be carried in a child seat. Seats are fitted mainly to the rear of the bike.
- **Trailers:** babies to five years *(up to two children).* Young babies can be strapped into their car seat and carried in a trailer, and older children can be strapped in and protected from the wind and rain.
- **Tag-along trailer bikes:** *approx four to nine years.* Tag-alongs (the back half of a child's bike attached to the back of an adult one) allow a child to be towed while they either add some of their own pedal power or just freewheel and enjoy the ride.
- **Tow bar:** *approx four to eight years.* A tow bar converts a standard child's bike to a trailer bike by lifting their front wheel from the ground to prevent them from steering, while enabling them to pedal independently. When you reach a safe place, the tow bar can be detached and the child's bike freed.

TEACHING YOUR CHILD TO RIDE

There are lots of ways for children to develop and gain cycling confidence before they head out on their own.

- **Tricycles or trikes:** available for children from ten months to five years old. They have pedals so kids have all the fun of getting around under their own steam.
- **Balance bikes:** are like normal bikes but without the pedals. This means children learn to balance, steer and gain confidence on two wheels while being able to place their feet firmly and safely on the ground.

- **Training wheels:** stabilisers give support to the rear of the bike and are the easiest way to learn to ride but potentially the slowest.

BUYING THE RIGHT BIKE FOR YOUR CHILD

Every child develops differently and they may be ready to learn to ride between the ages of three and seven. When children do progress to their own bike, emphasising the fun aspect will help them take the tumbles in their stride. Encouragement and praise are important to help them persevere.

Children's bikes generally fall into age categories based on the average size of a child of a specific age. There are no hard and fast rules, as long as your child isn't stretched and can reach the brakes safely and change gear easily. It's important to buy your child a bike that fits them rather than one they can grow into. Ask your local bike shop for advice and take your child along to try out different makes and sizes.

To find a specialist cycle retailer near you visit www.thecyclingexperts.co.uk

HOT TIPS & COOL TRICKS...

WHAT TO WEAR

For most of the rides featured in this book you do not need any special clothing or footwear. Shoes that are suitable for walking are also fine for cycling. Looser-fitting trousers allow your legs to move more freely, while tops with zips let you regulate your temperature. In cold weather, take gloves and a warm hat; it's also a good idea to pack a waterproof. If you are likely to be out at dusk, take a bright reflective top. If you start to cycle regularly, you may want to invest in some specialist equipment for longer rides, especially padded shorts and gloves.

WHAT TO TAKE

For a short ride, the minimum you will need is a pump and a small tool bag with a puncture repair kit, just in case. However, it is worth considering the following: water bottle, spare inner tube, 'multi-tool' (available from cycle shops), lock, money, sunglasses, lightweight waterproof (some pack down as small as a tennis ball), energy bars, map, camera and a spare top in case it cools down or to keep you warm when you stop for refreshments.

HOW TO TAKE IT

Rucksacks are fine for light loads but can make your back hot and sweaty. For heavier loads and for longer or more regular journeys, you are better off with panniers that attach to a bike rack.

BIKE ACCESSORIES

You may also want to invest in a helmet. A helmet will not prevent accidents from happening but can provide protection if you do fall off your bike. They are particularly recommended for young children. Ultimately, wearing a helmet is a question of individual choice and parents need to make that choice for their children.

A bell is a must for considerate cyclists. A friendly tinkle warns that you are approaching, but never assume others can hear you.

LOCKING YOUR BIKE

Unless you are sitting right next to your bike when you stop for refreshments, it is worth locking it, preferably to something immovable like a post, fence or railings (or a bike stand, of course). If nothing else, lock it to a companion's bike. Bike theft is more common in towns and cities, and if you regularly leave your bike on the streets, it is important to invest in a good-quality lock and to lock and leave your bike in a busy, well-lit location.

GETTING TO THE START OF A RIDE

The best rides are often those that you can do right from your doorstep, maximizing time on your bike and reducing travelling time. If you need to travel to the start of the ride, have you thought about catching a train?

FINDING OUT MORE – WWW.SUSTRANS.ORG.UK

Use the Sustrans website to find out where you can cycle to from home or while you are away on holiday, and browse through a whole host of other useful information.
Visit www.sustrans.org.uk

MAKING THE MOST OF YOUR BIKE

Making a few simple adjustments to your bike will make your ride more enjoyable and comfortable:

- **Saddle height:** raise or lower it so that you have good contact with your pedals (to make the most of your leg power) and so that you can always put a reassuring foot on the ground.
- **Saddle position:** getting the saddle in the right place will help you get the most from your pedal power without straining your body.
- **Handlebars:** well-positioned handlebars are crucial for your comfort and important for control of your steering and brakes.

...BIKE MAINTENANCE

Like any machine, a bike will work better and last longer if you care for it properly. Get in the habit of checking your bike regularly – simple checks and maintenance can help you have hassle-free riding and avoid repairs.

- **Tools:** there are specialist tools for specific tasks, but all you need to get started are: a pump, an old toothbrush, lubricants and grease, cleaning rags, a puncture repair kit, tyre levers, allen keys, screwdrivers and spanners.

REGULAR CHECKS

- **Every week:** Check tyres, brakes, lights, handlebars and seat are in good order and tightly secured.
- **Every month:** Wipe clean and lubricate chain with chain oil.
  Wipe the dirt from wheels.
  Check tread on tyres.
  Check brake pads.
  Check gear and brake cables and make sure that gears are changing smoothly.
- **Every year:** Take your bike to an experienced mechanic for a thorough service.
- **Tip:** If in doubt, leave it to the professionals. Bike mechanics are much more affordable than car mechanics, and some will even collect the bike from your home and return it to you when all the work is done.

FIXING A PUNCTURE

Punctures don't happen often and are easy to fix yourself. If you don't fancy repairing a puncture on your journey, carry a spare inner tube and a pump so you can change the tube, then fix the puncture when you get home. If you don't mind repairing punctures when they happen, make sure you carry your repair kit and pump with you at all times. All puncture repair kits have full instructions with easy-to-follow pictures.

Alternatively, if you don't want to get your hands dirty, just visit your local bike shop and they will fix the puncture for you.

Regular checks and inspections

Mending a puncture: easy peasy

Yearly professional checks and servicing

13

MILTON KEYNES & THE GRAND UNION CANAL

It may come as a surprise to some that there is an excellent network of recreational cycle routes in and around Milton Keynes, including circuits of lakes, tree-lined canal towpaths and well-made paths across parkland. Other surprises include a Buddhist pagoda and lots of adventure playgrounds. This route largely follows the course of the Grand Union Canal towpath from the centre of Milton Keynes, south to Leighton Buzzard and passing through Bletchley, which became famous as the headquarters of the Enigma code-breakers during World War II.

When integrated in 1929, the Grand Union Canal was an amalgam of at least eight separate canals, and of these the Grand Junction Canal from Braunston near Daventry to the Thames at Brentford, west of London, was by far the most important. Built in the late 18th century, it cut a full 60 miles (96.5km) off the canal journey between the Midlands and London – until then, the existing canal had joined the Thames at Oxford. In 1929, the various canals were integrated with the aim of establishing a 70-ton barge standard throughout the waterways of the Midlands, widening locks wherever necessary. However, the money ran out by 1932, the task remained unfinished and broad-beam boats never became common on the Grand Union Canal – many of the canals are still passable only by narrowboats, 2m (6.5ft) wide.

ROUTE INFORMATION
National Routes: 51, 6
Start: Milton Keynes Central train station.
Finish: Leighton Buzzard train station.
Distance: 16 miles (25.5km). Shorter option, from Bletchley to Leighton Buzzard; 7 miles (11km).
Grade: Easy.
Surface: Tarmac.
Hills: None.

Cows in the Milton Keynes shopping centre

YOUNG & INEXPERIENCED CYCLISTS
In Milton Keynes, all busy roads are crossed via underpasses or bridges. There are on-road sections south of Woughton on the Green and through Bletchley, but these are all minor roads. As an alternative, the ride can be started at Bletchley, following the towpath all the way to Leighton Buzzard.

REFRESHMENTS
- Lots of choice in the square by the train station and elsewhere in central Milton Keynes.
- Good picnic spots at Willen Lakeside Park (just off the route) and Caldecotte Lake.
- Ye Olde Swan pub and shop in Woughton on the Green (just off the route).
- Caldecotte Arms (windmill pub) by Caldecotte Lake.

Narrowboat on the Grand Union Canal

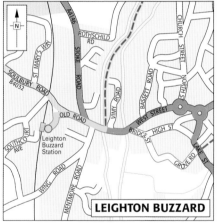
LEIGHTON BUZZARD

- The Grand Union pub at Stoke Hammond and Globe Inn at Linslade (both on towpath).

THINGS TO SEE & DO
- **Peace Pagoda, Willen Lakeside Park:** just off the route; the first of its kind in the West, with a frieze telling the story of the Buddha; a Circle of Hearts Medicine Wheel (a Native American stone circle and symbol of peace); and Tim Minett and Neil Higson's turf maze with bronze roundels representing the four races of mankind. www.mkparks.co.uk
- **Walton Lake nature reserve:** just off the route; has the city's largest reed beds. www.mkparks.co.uk
- **Children's play area near Caldecotte Arms:** (windmill pub) by Caldecotte Lake; www.mkparks.co.uk
- **Ancient churches of St Mary's at Woughton and St Thomas's at Simpson:** www.woughton.org/churches
- **Leighton Buzzard:** this charming old market town is well worth exploring.

TRAIN STATIONS
Milton Keynes Central; Bow Brickhill; Fenny Stratford; Bletchley; Leighton Buzzard.

BIKE HIRE
- **Willen Lake:** 01908 691616

FURTHER INFORMATION
- To view or print National Cycle Network routes, visit www.sustrans.org.uk
- Maps for this area available to buy from www.sustransshop.co.uk
- **Milton Keynes Tourist Information:** 01908 677010; www.destinationmiltonkeynes.co.uk

ROUTE DESCRIPTION
Go straight ahead from Milton Keynes Central station and follow Route 51 along Midsummer

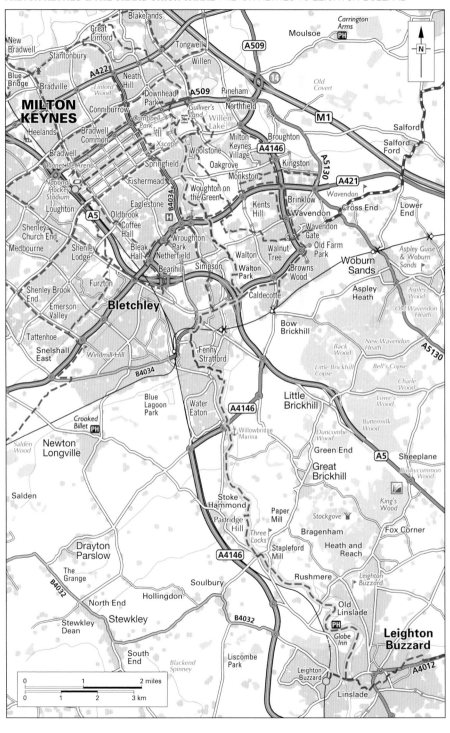

The Globe Inn near Leighton Buzzard

Peace Pagoda at Willen Lakeside Park

Beacon Point in Campbell Park

Boulevard. Cross the overbridge into Campbell Park, where there are splendid views of the surrounding countryside. Keep following the Route 51 signs until you meet Route 6 at the canal. For a short detour, continue straight on, following Route 51 to Willen Lakeside Park, which offers a good picnic spot and a chance to explore the Peace Pagoda, Circle of Hearts Medicine Wheel and turf maze.

To continue on the ride, return to the canal and Route 6 and follow the towpath south towards Woughton on the Green. There is a short section on minor roads through Woughton when you pass close to the Open University. The 13th-century church of St Mary's and the Walton Lake nature reserve are also both close by. (Walton Lake was dried out when it was no longer needed to cope with floodwater, which is now taken by Willen and Caldecotte Lakes.) At Simpson, where there is another 13th-century church, join the path alongside the River Ouzel – companion waterway to the canal – and cycle past Caldecotte Lake, another good picnic spot, with its windmill pub and children's play area.

The route follows minor roads through Bletchley before rejoining the canal towpath

for 6 miles (9.5km), all the way to Leighton Buzzard. Here, you could visit the Georgian high street and market square before turning back to the station (all are within easy reach of the canal towpath).

NEARBY CYCLE ROUTES
The section of this ride that goes through Milton Keynes is part of the 170-mile (273km) Redway network, named after its red tarmac surface, with routes throughout the town.

Milton Keynes is at a crossroads of the National Cycle Network. Route 6 passes through Milton Keynes on its way south from Leicester and Northampton to St Albans and London. Route 51 runs from Oxford to Bedford, Cambridge and the east coast.

PHOENIX TRAIL

Passing through the countryside on the border between Oxfordshire and Buckinghamshire, the Phoenix Trail links the attractive market towns of Thame and Princes Risborough, providing an ideal traffic-free ride for novice cyclists and families with young children. Sit on the sculptures, which are dotted along the trail, to admire the magnificent views of the nearby Chiltern Hills and observe red kites, the impressive birds of prey that thrive in the area. Keep an eye out for the sculptures of strange animals perched high up on poles about halfway along the ride.

Running along the base of the Chilterns southwest from Bledlow, near the Princes Risborough end of the ride, is the Ridgeway; a reasonably level, broad, stone and chalk track that offers easy off-road riding for mountain bikes through the summer and early autumn. This ancient trading route is over 5,000 years old and claimed to be the oldest in Europe. It used to link the flint workings at Grime's Graves in Norfolk with the Dorset coast. The Chilterns themselves are criss-crossed with bridleways and byways, and also offer excellent mountain biking, but obviously the rides are a lot tougher than the Phoenix Trail.

ROUTE INFORMATION
National Route: 57
Start: Princes Risborough train station.
Finish: Upper High Street, Thame.
Distance: 7 miles (11km).
Grade: Easy.
Surface: Part tarmac, part limestone dust.
Hills: None.

YOUNG & INEXPERIENCED CYCLISTS
The route allows you to enjoy the countryside without tackling hills or long distances. There is a 1.25-mile (2km) section on-road from Princes Risborough to Horsenden, where the 6-mile (9.5km) traffic-free path starts and goes all the way to Thame.

REFRESHMENTS
- Lots of choice in Princes Risborough.
- Red Lion pub at Longwick, just off the route.
- Three Horseshoes pub at Towersey.
- Lots of choice in Thame.

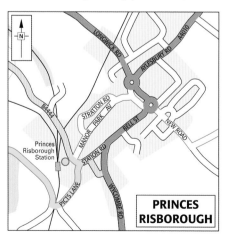

PRINCES RISBOROUGH

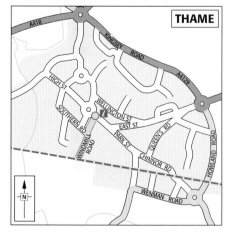

THAME

THINGS TO SEE & DO

- **Princes Risborough:** market town with a history stretching back over 5,500 years.
- **Thame:** historic market town with an attractive centre and unique shops.
- Look out for a rich variety of wildlife, including red kites.
- There is a wide selection of artworks along the route.

TRAIN STATIONS

Princes Risborough.

BIKE HIRE

- Risborough Cycles, Princes Risborough: 01844 345949; www.risboroughcycles.com

FURTHER INFORMATION

- To view or print National Cycle Network routes, visit www.sustrans.org.uk
- Maps for this area are available to buy from www.sustransshop.co.uk
- Princes Risborough Tourist Information: 01844 274795; www.visitbuckinghamshire.org
- Thame Tourist Information: 01844 212833; www.visitsouthoxfordshire.co.uk

St Mary's Church at Thame

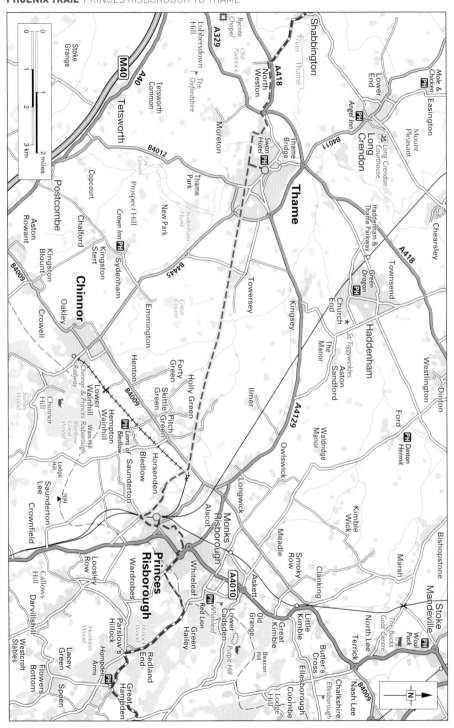

The red kite is often seen in the Chilterns

ROUTE DESCRIPTION

From Princes Risborough, after leaving the station approach road, follow the National Cycle Network Route 57 signs to the start of the traffic-free path in Horsenden.

The route is then traffic-free all the way to Thame and passes through the countryside on the border between Oxfordshire and Buckinghamshire. The terrain is largely flat, but the Chilterns make an impressive backdrop to the ride towards Thame.

The market towns of Princes Risborough and Thame are both worth a potter, so add in extra time to your ride.

NEARBY CYCLE ROUTES

National Route 57 continues, mainly on-road, west of Thame to Oxford: go past Lord Williams's School and follow the signs.

For the more energetic, the Ridgeway (a national walking trail and Britain's oldest road) is nearby, and a 9-mile (14.5km) section west of Bledlow is open to cyclists.

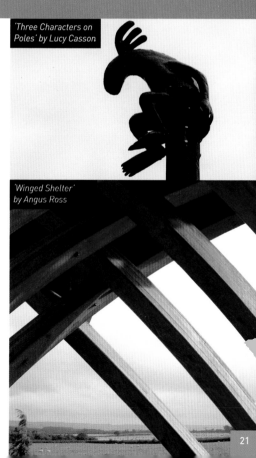

'Three Characters on Poles' by Lucy Casson

'Winged Shelter' by Angus Ross

THE HANSON WAY

Oxford is a cycling city, and you certainly feel you are with kindred spirits as you pedal around its streets. So, at the start of this ride, you might like to cycle past a few of the colleges along Broad Street and Catte Street, to soak up the atmosphere of this historic city before leaving to join the River Thames. The towpath is as good a route as it gets, with the added excitement of rowers on the water and their coaches cycling blindly along the bank, where you are expected to get out of their way. Sustrans had hopes to continue along the riverside towpath all the way to Abingdon, but it was not to be, at least for the moment.

In complete contrast with the beginning of the ride, at the end you are dwarfed by the vast cooling towers of Didcot Power Station, essential technology for our times, but one whose profligacy you are challenging by cycling today.

A welcome break on the Hanson Way

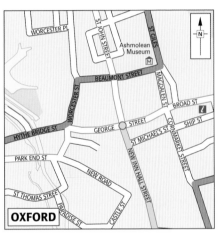

OXFORD

ROUTE INFORMATION

National Route: 5
Start: George Street, Oxford.
Finish: Didcot Parkway train station.
Distance: 15 miles (24km).
Grade: Easy.
Surface: Stone paths and tarmac roads.
Hills: Almost entirely flat.

YOUNG & INEXPERIENCED CYCLISTS

The whole route is easy to ride, provided you take care on one or two of the road sections. The best section for families is the riverside route in Oxford down as far as the Kennington meadows.

REFRESHMENTS

• Lots of choice in Oxford and Didcot.

• Isis Tavern, The Towing Path, Oxford.
• The Tandem pub, Kennington.
• The Bowyer Arms, Radley, near the train station.
• Cafes and pubs on Stert Street in Abingdon town centre.

THINGS TO SEE & DO

• **Oxford University:** take a look around the magnificent grounds of one of the most famous universities in the world; 01865 726871; www.ox.ac.uk
• **Christ Church Cathedral, Oxford:** Oxford University's largest college and the cathedral church for the Anglican Diocese of Oxford, originally founded in 1524 by Cardinal

Wolsey; 01865 276150; www.chch.ox.ac.uk
- **Punting on the Thames, Oxford:** explore the river in a punt, rowing boat or canoe; 01865 515978; www.cherwellboathouse.co.uk
- **Pendon Museum, Long Wittenham:** indoor miniature model village and railways, capturing England in the 1930s; 01865 407365; www.pendonmuseum.com
- **Abingdon Museum:** housed in the

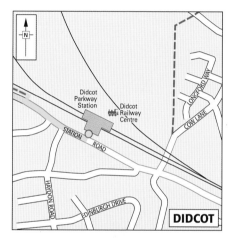

magnificent former County Hall (1684), includes natural history exhibits and a selection of crafts from the former Southern Arts Collection; 01235 539794; www.abingdonmuseum.org.uk
- **Didcot Railway Centre:** based around an original 1930s engine shed and featuring a collection of Great Western Railway steam engines, coaches, wagons and a recreation of Brunel's broad-gauge railway; 01235 817200; www.didcotrailwaycentre.org.uk

TRAIN STATIONS
Oxford; Radley; Didcot Parkway.

BIKE HIRE
- **Cycloanalysts, Oxford:** 01865 424444; www.cycloanalysts.com
- **Bike Zone, Oxford:** 01865 728877; www.bike-zone.co.uk
- **Pedal Power, Abingdon:** 01235 525123

FURTHER INFORMATION
- To view or print National Cycle Network routes, visit www.sustrans.org.uk

Punting by Magdalen Bridge, Oxford

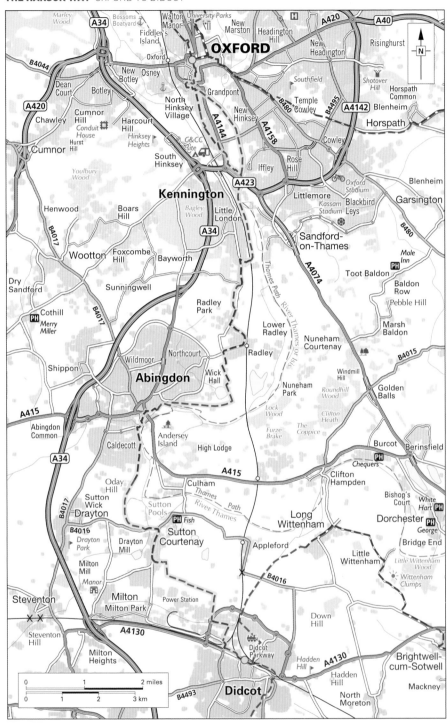

Oxford's Radcliffe
Camera building

Oxford's Bridge
of Sighs

- Maps for this area are available to buy from www.sustransshop.org.uk
- **Oxford Tourist Information:** 01865 726871; www.visitoxford.andoxfordshire.com

ROUTE DESCRIPTION

George Street is as central a spot as you can find, but if you lose your way in the maze of streets, just remember you are heading for the towpath that runs along the south side of the Thames. You start by going down New Inn Hall Street, which is usually crowded with shoppers and students. Follow this to Bonn Square, near Oxford Library, and then down St Ebbes Street, a quiet backwater that leads you through to a crossing of the main road and eventually a bridge over the Thames. Here, the official National Route 5 is signposted southwards on minor roads but, as a visitor, you should turn left and follow the Thames towpath, past boathouses and the delightful Isis Tavern, which is accessible only from the towpath. Continue on the towpath until you eventually pass under a railway bridge and leave the riverside, to cross the meadows for a path beside the railway to reach Sandford Lane. Turn right here and left onto Kennington Road, where after half a mile (0.8km) you join a cycle track along the right-hand side of the road.

Cycle past Radley College and turn left to Radley station (all signed). Coming away from the station, turn left at the crossroads onto a farm road leading down to gravel pits, where the route becomes traffic-free again, past lakes and onto the old Abingdon branch line into town. You emerge under an archway between the Civic Centre and St Nicholas' Church and run past the Abingdon Museum situated in an historic building. You are now on the riverside again. Carry on south past the inevitable sewage works for Peep-O-Day Lane and the route into Sutton Courtenay. Turn right here along the High Street. Be careful to bear left at the end, into Frilsham Street, where the houses are overshadowed by Didcot Power Station. Continue on Route 5 into Didcot.

NEARBY CYCLE ROUTES

From Oxford, National Route 5 continues northwards on the towpath of the Oxford Canal and makes a good route to Blenheim Palace, 7 miles (11km) away. From Didcot, Route 5 to Reading doubles back northwards through the Wittenhams for Wallingford and a route through the Chilterns. South of Didcot, the route to Upton and Wantage gives you the opportunity to pick up that most ancient of roads, the Ridgeway.

DIDCOT, WANTAGE & RIDGEWAY

This route gives you an introduction to the Ridgeway, commonly known as Britain's oldest road and certainly in use since Neolithic times. The formal route runs for some 87 miles (140km), from Overton Hill near Avebury to Ivinghoe Beacon near Aylesbury. Originally, though, it would almost certainly have followed the dry chalk uplands all the way from Dorset to Lincolnshire.

The 11 miles (17.5km) featured here are magnificently perched on the north edge of the downlands, with far-flung views over the Thames Valley and Didcot Power Station, known as the Cathedral of the Vale.

This ride is based around Regional Route 44, which runs mostly traffic-free from Didcot to Wantage along the foot of the hills. From here, there are numerous ways up to the Ridgeway, all of which deserve exploring – there are too many to describe in this guide.

If you have never ventured off tarmac, then this is your chance to cycle on far older surfaces – gravel, chalk and even grass. The ground is generally dry and, although you might go a little faster on a mountain bike, the route is suitable for everyone.

ROUTE INFORMATION
National Route: 5
Regional Route: 44
Start: Didcot Parkway train station.
Finish: Didcot Parkway train station.
Distance: Didcot to Wantage 11 miles (17.5km). Loop via East Hendred Down 18 miles (29km); longer loop via Wantage 32 miles (51.5km).
Grade: Medium.
Surface: The surface does vary a great deal. The Ridgeway becomes hard to use in the depths of winter, when the ground has had no chance to dry out.
Hills: Although there is a climb up to the Ridgeway, this ride is not particularly hilly.

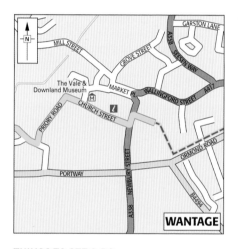

WANTAGE

YOUNG & INEXPERIENCED CYCLISTS
The Upton Railway path is particularly suitable for children and the whole way to Wantage is a good adventure for novices.

REFRESHMENTS
- Lots of choice in Didcot and Wantage.
- Ridgeway Cafe, Didcot.
- Didcot Arts Centre cafe.
- Kingswell Hotel, Harwell, west of Didcot.
- George and Dragon pub, Upton.

THINGS TO SEE & DO
- **Didcot Railway Centre:** based around an original 1930s engine shed and featuring a collection of Great Western Railway steam engines, coaches, wagons and a recreation of Brunel's broad-gauge railway; 01235 817200; www.didcotrailwaycentre.org.uk
- **Vale & Downland Museum, Wantage:** a look at the cultural heritage of the Vale of the White Horse region; 01235 771447; www.wantage.com/museum/

'Spiralling Steam' by
Rob Woods

King Alfred the
Great, Wantage

The track at
Wantage

TRAIN STATIONS
Didcot Parkway.

BIKE HIRE
None locally.

FURTHER INFORMATION
- To view or print National Cycle Network routes, visit www.sustrans.org.uk
- Maps for this area are available to buy from www.sustransshop.co.uk

ROUTE DESCRIPTION
Turn left from Didcot Parkway train station and follow the cycle route along the side of the main road to the Broadway roundabout. Here, use the two sets of toucan crossing lights to reach the railway path. The route then runs towards Upton, with one or two small deviations where the line has been lost. Past East Hagbourne, the line climbs on a high embankment to give you a dramatic approach to the Downs on the horizon. Go west in Upton and follow roads up to Hagbourne Hill. Here, you join a gravel road, leave the telecommunications mast to your left, cross over the main road on a farm bridge and then go straight to cross the Harwell Road at the traffic lights. The route now follows the old Icknield track at the bottom of the hill. Don't worry about the military-looking blockhouse built across the way – just go round it!

At the East Hendred Road, the signed route turns left and then right down a grand avenue to East Ginge (or go straight on for the shorter loop; see below). Now follow the lanes all the way to West Lockinge to pick up the track

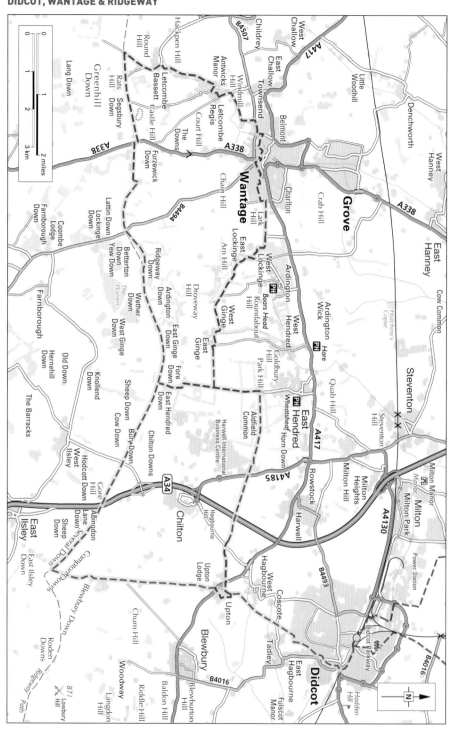

Mill Street, Wantage

again, which is now surfaced, to Wantage. For the short Ridgeway loop, climb up the tarmac road from East Hendred to the top of the Downs and you will see the Ridgeway stretching away to the east. It is a mixture of chalk or gravel, of grass and even narrow earth surfaces, but the ground drains so well that you can generally make excellent progress, especially if the wind is on your back. After the main road bridge, the Ridgeway runs beside and crosses horse gallops and you sense a different world approaching. On a clear day, you have stupendous views out northwards to Oxford and across the wide downlands, with the Fair Mile trackway snaking away in the distance. Just before the Ridgeway itself turns sharp left, you turn left and drop steeply down to the old railway bridge and the long straight road to Upton – partly tarmac, partly concrete, partly grass and ending in the Hollow Way. Cross the main road with care and rejoin the railway path to Didcot.

NEARBY CYCLE ROUTES

There is a longer Ridgeway loop, 32 miles (51.5km), that continues through Wantage, past Market Place and the Vale & Downland Museum and down Water Lane for a footbridge crossing of the stream if you don't fancy the ford. There, you turn off the B4507 for Letcombe Regis. From Didcot, you can follow Route 5 northwards to Abingdon and Oxford, or to Long Wittenham for Reading. If your appetite for gravel routes remains unabated, you can explore the Little Wittenham crossing of the Thames to Dorchester.

KENNET & AVON CANAL

The Kennet & Avon Cycle Route runs for 100 miles (161km) from the centre of Bristol to the centre of Reading. This ride follows the last 20 miles (32km) from Newbury, introducing you to the pleasures of slipping through the countryside from one town to another with scarcely more contact with traffic than the groan of the M4 in the distance and the occasional road crossing.

Newbury, for all its charm, has been the scene of some key protests in recent years. Nearby Greenham Common will forever be remembered as the focus of the so-called Peace Women's protest in the 1980s against American nuclear weapons being based there, while Swampy made his name in the 1990s protesting against the planned Newbury bypass. You, too, by cycling, rather than driving, can add to this proud tradition with your gentle campaign for more sustainable transport.

ROUTE INFORMATION
National Route: 4
Start: Newbury Bridge.
Finish: Reading train station.
Distance: 20 miles (32km).
Grade: Easy.
Surface: Mostly compacted stone.
Hills: Entirely level, except for canal bridges.

YOUNG & INEXPERIENCED CYCLISTS
The route is almost entirely traffic-free, except for a section through Thatcham, which can be bypassed by the towpath, albeit of a rougher standard. It is suitable for novices and families, as the return journey can be made by train.

REFRESHMENTS
- Lots of choice in Reading.
- Cafe Uno, Newbury.
- Old Waggon & Horses pub, Newbury.
- The Stone Building cafe, Newbury Wharf.
- Cafe in Aldermaston Wharf by the canal.

THINGS TO SEE & DO
- Highclere Castle, south of Newbury: Victorian castle and gardens; features an extensive Egyptian antiquities exhibition of

Bulls Lock at Thatcham

items collected by Lord Carnarvon, who discovered the tomb of Tutankhamun; 01635 253210; www.highclerecastle.co.uk

- **West Berkshire Brewery:** based in Frilsham and Yattendon, supplying quality beer to local pubs; also a brewery shop; 01635 202968; www.wbbrew.com

- **Thatcham Millennium Monument on the Broadway:** illustrates Thatcham's place in the Guinness Book of Records as the oldest continuously inhabited place in England; www.thatchamtowncouncil.gov.uk

- **Reading Museum:** diverse exhibitions ranging from a copy of the Bayeux Tapestry to biscuit tins; 0118 937 3400; www.readingmuseum.org.uk

TRAIN STATIONS

Newbury; Thatcham; Midgham; Aldermaston; Theale; Reading.

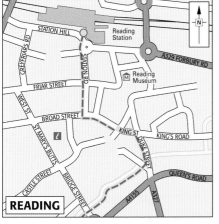

Newbury to Thatcham towpath

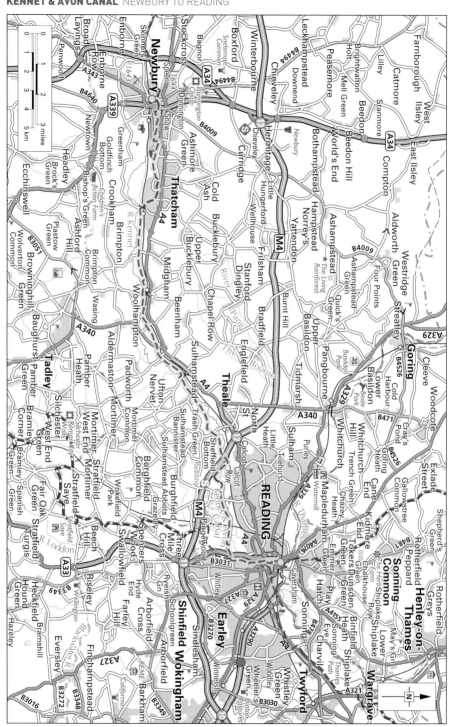

The grand façade of Highclere Castle

FURTHER INFORMATION

- To view or print National Cycle Network routes, visit www.sustrans.org.uk
- Maps for this area are available to buy from www.sustransshop.org.uk
- **British Waterways:** 01923 201120; www.waterscape.com

ROUTE DESCRIPTION

Start at Newbury Bridge at the end of Northbrook Street. Newbury Wharf, the Information Centre, the Town Museum and station are all just over the canal to the south. Follow the towpath eastwards, signed National Route 4. This navigation is part river, part canal, and the towpath flips from side to side as various watercourses converge or part. Each time, you have a pretty little bridge to take you over the water and provide you with views up and down the waterway.

At Hambridge Road Bridge – the first road you come to – the signed route turns away to the left to pass through Thatcham, which has the distinction of being considered the oldest continuously occupied place in England. Some notable dates in the town's history are listed on the Millennium Monument just to your left on the Broadway. You rejoin the canal at Thatcham train station. Note that cycling is permitted on

the towpath from Hambridge Road to this point, although the surface is not so good. You might want to see Monkey Marsh Lock just upstream of Thatcham, one of only two turf-sided locks in the country. You now follow the canal towpath beyond the M4 near Reading. Near Woolhampton, there is a short section in private ownership where you should walk, and just beyond Sulhamstead Lock, the path is unsurfaced across a couple of fields with particular wildlife interest. Beyond the M4, bear away from the towpath for a little way and, once past Fobney Lock and under the A33, cycle on either side of the Kennet to Reading town centre. The best way to reach Reading train station is probably to leave the canal at Duke Street, just beyond the Oracle Shopping Complex, turn left at King Street and follow pedestrian streets (dismount where necessary) and bus lanes to the station.

NEARBY CYCLE ROUTES

National Route 4 stretches west towards Devizes, Bath, Bristol and Fishguard, while at Reading you can continue to London on a route that, once past Windsor and Staines, largely follows the banks of the Thames. Route 5 to Oxford climbs hills around Sonning Common before re-crossing the Thames at Wallingford.

THE JUBILEE RIVER – MAIDENHEAD, WINDSOR & SLOUGH

This ride is a hub spinning off interesting links in all directions, all under the distant gaze of Windsor Castle and the surveillance of planes flying into Heathrow. It passes the Fat Duck in Bray, possibly the most renowned restaurant in England, Dorney Lake rowing centre, venue for some of the 2012 Olympic events, past Eton College and Windsor Castle, and then back along the Jubilee River. Opened in 2002 to celebrate the Queen's Golden Jubilee, this wide, 7-mile (11km) long waterway was dug to divert flood waters on the Thames. What more could be concentrated into this small but wonderfully open space, apart from the Thames, of course, and Brunel's renowned Maidenhead Bridge? This is a little ride with lots to take home at the end of the day.

A swan on the Thames at Windsor

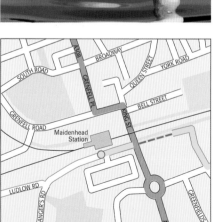
MAIDENHEAD

ROUTE INFORMATION
National Routes: 4, 61
Start: Maidenhead train station.
Finish: Maidenhead train station.
Distance: 16 miles (25.5km).
Grade: Easy.
Surface: Minor tarmac roads; elsewhere, mostly stone.
Hills: The only climbs are bridges over the Thames.

YOUNG & INEXPERIENCED CYCLISTS
The whole route is suitable for novices and families, although care is needed at the end of the ride back to Maidenhead if you take the A4 option.

REFRESHMENTS
• Lots of choice in Maidenhead and Eton.
• The Crown Inn, Bray.
• Cafe at Walled Garden Centre, Dorney Court.
• The Palmer Arms pub, Dorney.
• The Three Horseshoes, Eton Wick.

THINGS TO SEE & DO
• St Michael's Church, Bray: historic church dating back to 1293; 01628 633113; www.braystmichael.co.uk
• Dorney Lake Park: rowing venue for the 2012 Olympics, set around Eton College Rowing Lake; 01753 832756; www.dorneylake.co.uk

Eton College clock

Fat Duck restaurant sign at Bray

- **Eton College, Eton:** founded in 1440 by Henry VI to provide free education for 70 pupils; 01753 671000; www.etoncollege.com
- **Windsor Castle:** largest inhabited castle in the world and the Queen's favourite weekend home; 020 7766 7304; www.windsor.gov.uk
- **Horse-drawn carriage rides through Windsor Great Park, Windsor:** 07811 543019
- **Legoland, Windsor:** family-focused theme park featuring rides and attractions based around the Lego toy; 0871 222 2001; www.legoland.co.uk

TRAIN STATIONS

Maidenhead; Windsor & Eton Central; Windsor & Eton Riverside; Slough.

BIKE HIRE

- **Windsor Cycle Hire:** 01753 830220
- **Stows Cycles, Windsor:** 01753 520528; www.stows.co.uk

FURTHER INFORMATION

- To view or print National Cycle Network routes, visit www.sustrans.org.uk
- Maps for this area are available to buy from www.sustransshop.org.uk
- **Royal Windsor & Maidenhead Tourist Information:** 01753 743900; www.windsor.gov.uk

ROUTE DESCRIPTION

Leave from the south side of Maidenhead train station, turn left and cross the main road at the traffic lights. Wriggle through the car park, turn

The turrets of Windsor Castle

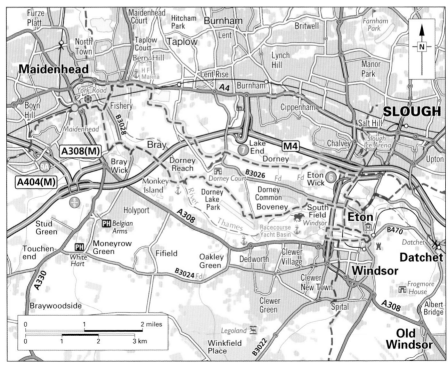

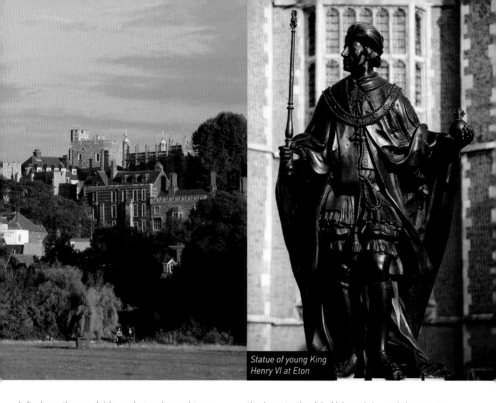

Statue of young King Henry VI at Eton

left along the roadside cycle tracks and turn right for a woodland ride to Bray. Continue through the village on a fairly busy road, bear left at the hotel and climb over the M4. Soon, turn left to cross the Thames on a bridge that used to carry the sand and gravel away from what is now the Eton rowing lake. Straight ahead is one of the links to the Jubilee River, but you turn right or, if it's not busy, go alongside the rowing lake. Beyond the club house, join the lane to Boveney Lock. Here, the riverside path leads through to run beside the Eton Wick Road, where there is another link to the Jubilee River, and under the Windsor railway viaduct. Turn left for the Jubilee River, and Slough, or right for a loop around the river and the traffic-free Eton Bridge over the Thames. Stop here for treats, visits to the castle or catch the train home.

Returning to the Jubilee River, you can turn east for landscaped Ditton Park and the Slough branch of the Grand Union Canal, or west for the wide expanses of the Jubilee River. At its Maidenhead end, cross the Jubilee and follow

the lane to the A4. Although busy, it is easy to ride in this direction going westwards, and children could use the footway. Just before Maidenhead Bridge over the Thames, turn left for the riverside and a closer look at Brunel's design, or carry on over the river, take the first left and cut through to Oldfield Road. Go straight across at the T-junction. After crossing the river, turn right on the original route back to Maidenhead station.

NEARBY CYCLE ROUTES

National Route 4 continues westwards to Reading, while eastwards it goes through Windsor Great Park to Staines for a largely riverside route to London (see pages 38 and 42). If you go past Ditton Park, Route 61 takes you to Uxbridge for the Grand Union Canal to Watford (see page 52).

STAINES TO HAMPTON COURT

At Staines, the Thames Cycle Route from Oxford finally joins the riverside path. Up to now it has touched on the Thames, looked over the Thames, but more often followed lanes and paths that wandered away from the river itself. But from Staines you can cycle almost all the way along the banks of the Thames to Hampton Court, and then follow it for sections to Westminster, Tower Bridge, Greenwich and Erith. Almost every part of the way is of interest and a pleasure. Numerous railway stations allow trips for every ambition and ability. It is a truly memorable way to approach London.

This section from Staines to Hampton Court Palace makes for an easy introduction to the Thames, with the added pleasure of the ferry crossing at Shepperton. Before you start downstream, a short detour upstream to Runnymede would take you to the site of King John's meeting with the barons and the signing of the Magna Carta.

From Shepperton, all along the river to Hampton, watch out for coaches cycling alongside their elegant rowing crews, exhorting and cajoling but taking very little notice of anyone else at all, including you! There are a number of pubs and refreshments along the river, such as Ye Olde Swan and The Weir, but, hopefully, despite them all, you will reach Hampton Court with energy to spare to look around this magnificent palace, first built by Cardinal Wolsey, Henry VIII's lord chancellor, and designed to show foreign ambassadors that he could live as graciously as any cardinal in Rome.

ROUTE INFORMATION

National Route: 4
Start: Staines train station.
Finish: Hampton Court Palace.
Distance: 13 miles (21km).
Grade: Easy.
Surface: Mixture of tarmac and good-quality gravel paths.
Hills: None.

YOUNG & INEXPERIENCED CYCLISTS

Most of the route is traffic-free, except for a short section where you follow the road to Shepperton via cycle lanes and shared footways.

REFRESHMENTS

- Lots of choice in Staines.
- The Orangery Cafe, Shepperton.
- Caffe Piccolo, Weybridge.
- The Weir pub, Walton-on-Thames.
- The Swan pub, Thames Ditton.
- Restaurants and cafes at Hampton Court Palace.

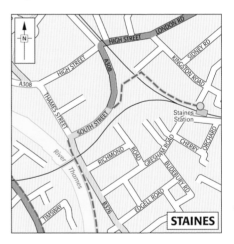

THINGS TO SEE & DO

- **Hampton Court Palace:** Tudor palace alongside a baroque palace, steeped in history; attractions include a maze, privy gardens, medieval hall and working Tudor kitchens; 0844 482 7777; www.hrp.org.uk

Hampton Court Palace entrance

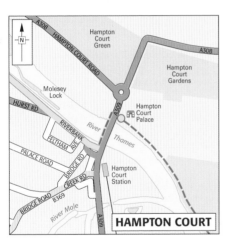

HAMPTON COURT

Cycling on the Thames Path

- **Shepperton Marina**: passenger ferries run to Weybridge, Hampton Court and Staines between Easter and 1 October; 01932 253374

TRAIN STATIONS
Staines; Shepperton; Addlestone; Hampton Court; Kingston.

FERRIES
Shepperton Ferry sails from just beyond Shepperton Lock at the end of Ferry Lane across to Weybridge; every 15 mins until 6pm in summer, 5pm in winter: 01932 254844

BIKE HIRE
- Birdie Bikes, Chertsey: 01932 560760; www.birdiebikes.co.uk

FURTHER INFORMATION
- To view or print National Cycle Network routes, visit www.sustrans.org.uk
- Maps for this area are available to buy from www.sustransshop.co.uk
- Kingston upon Thames Tourist Information: 020 8547 5592; www.kingston.gov.uk

ROUTE DESCRIPTION
Turn left out of the main entrance of Staines train station and proceed along a wide path by the railway and under the first bridge. A short ride through the town centre leads to the riverside. Turn left and follow the river

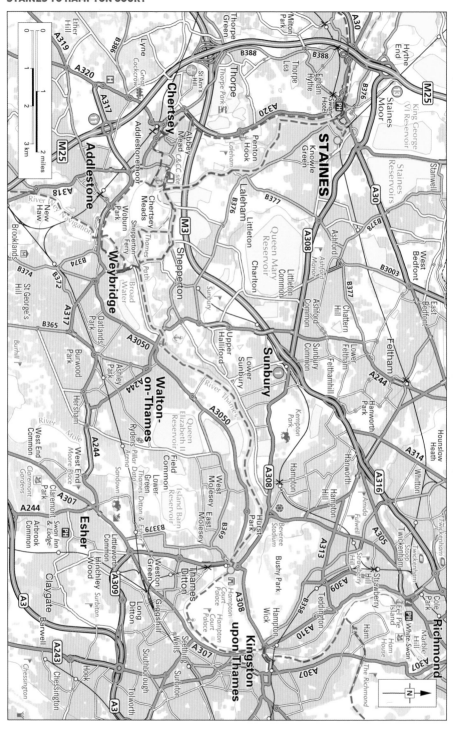

Brick chimneys at
Hampton Court Palace

downstream. Join the quiet road at Laleham,
all the way to Chertsey Bridge. Turn left at the
bridge and follow the cycle lane towards
Shepperton. After the roundabout, you can use
the shared path on the north side of the road.
After 600m (659 yards), turn right down a
narrow lane to the riverside and Shepperton
Ferry. (Note that if this is closed, you must
continue to Shepperton and rejoin the riverside
path at Walton Bridge.) From here it is a
riverside route all the way to Hampton Bridge
and the Palace. Watch out for the boathouses
along the way and also the fragile racing boats
as they are carried to and from the water. On
busy days you must wait for them.

NEARBY CYCLE ROUTES

National Route 4 continues west to Reading via
Windsor and Maidenhead (see page 34). To the
east, it continues via Richmond Park and the
Thames to Putney (see page 42). At Shepperton
Ferry, you can follow Route 4 signs to the start
of the River Wey Navigation and a towpath
route, to its junction with the Basingstoke
Canal, Brookwood and beyond (see page 62).

The Thames Path in
Hampton Court Park

HAMPTON COURT TO PUTNEY

Forming part of Route 4, which runs all the way from West Wales to the capital, this splendid green and leafy corridor offers plenty of interest, including Hampton Court Palace, boating at Teddington Lock, deer in Richmond Park and the Wetland Centre at Barnes. The Palace was originally built for Cardinal Wolsey but it passed to Henry VIII when he fell out of favour with the king. It was at Hampton Court Palace that the King James Bible had its origins and, during the Civil War, Charles I was held prisoner here for three months before escaping. There is a striking contrast between the wide, untamed tidal Thames from Putney Bridge as far west as Teddington Lock, and the highly managed pleasure boat section that lies beyond.

Just off the route but connected to Route 4 via traffic-free paths are the Royal Botanic Gardens at Kew and Ham House, owned by the National Trust. Kew Gardens were started in 1759 by Princess Augusta, the mother of George III. They now cover more than 300 acres, and contain over 25,000 species and varieties of plants, as well as statues, glasshouses and an 18th-century pagoda. Ham House is a 17th-century mansion famous for its decorative interiors and restored formal gardens.

ROUTE INFORMATION
National Route: 4
Start: Hampton Court Palace.
Finish: Putney Bridge, south bank.
Distance: 12 miles (19.5km). Shorter options: from Hampton Court Palace to Richmond Park 6 miles (9.5km); from Hampton Court Palace to Kingston upon Thames 3 miles (5km).
Grade: Easy.
Surface: Mixture of tarmac and good-quality gravel paths.
Hills: Mostly level with a gentle rolling section through Richmond Park.

YOUNG & INEXPERIENCED CYCLISTS
The route is a mixture of quiet streets and cyclepaths. The best traffic-free section alongside the river runs from Hampton Court to Kingston Bridge.

REFRESHMENTS
• Lots of choice all along the ride.

THINGS TO SEE & DO

- **Hampton Court Palace:** Tudor palace alongside a baroque palace, steeped in history; attractions include a maze, privy gardens, medieval hall and working Tudor kitchens; 0844 482 7777; www.hrp.org.uk
- **Ham House, Ham:** Stuart mansion and gardens on the banks of the River Thames; 17th-century interiors and collections of textiles, furniture and paintings; reputedly the most haunted house in England; 020 8940 1950; www.nationaltrust.org.uk
- **Richmond Park:** the largest Royal Park in London and home to around 650 free-roaming deer; designated a National Nature Reserve (NNR), a Site of Special Scientific Interest (SSSI) and a Special Area of Conservation (SAC); 0300 061 2000; www.royalparks.org.uk
- **Royal Botanic Gardens, Kew:** just off the route; 020 8332 5655; www.kew.org
- **The National Archives, Kew:** just off the route; contains almost 1,000 years of history; 020 8876 3444; www.nationalarchives.gov.uk
- **Wildfowl & Wetlands Trust (WWT), Barnes:** 020 8409 4400; www.wwt.org.uk

Herd of deer in Richmond Park

Palm House at Royal Botanic Gardens, Kew

TRAIN STATIONS
Hampton Court; Hampton Wick; Kingston; Barnes; Putney.

BIKE HIRE
- **Go Pedal!:** delivery to most areas of London; 07850 796320; www.gopedal.co.uk
- **London Bicycle Tour Company, Gabriel's Wharf:** 020 7928 6838; www.londonbicycle.com
- **Smith Brothers, Wimbledon:** 020 8946 2270

FURTHER INFORMATION
- To view or print National Cycle Network routes, visit www.sustrans.org.uk
- Maps for this area are available to buy from www.sustransshop.co.uk
- **Transport for London Cycle Guides:** free guides covering Greater London, with routes recommended by experienced cyclists; 0843 222 1234; www.tfl.gov.uk/cycling
- **Transport for London Journey Planner:** detailed information to help you plan your travel anywhere in Greater London, by bike, on foot or on public transport; 0843 222 1234; www.tfl.gov.uk
- **London Cycling Campaign:** provides information and advice on cycling in London; 020 7234 9310; www.lcc.org.uk

- **London Tourist Information:** 08701 566 366; www.visitlondon.com

ROUTE DESCRIPTION
Starting at Hampton Court Park, travel along Barge Walk and cross Kingston Bridge, near Kingston train station, and where there is a good cycle route. Follow the Route 4 signs through Kingston upon Thames and along the river to Teddington Lock.

At Teddington Lock, leave the river to go straight through Richmond Park, or complete a traffic-free circuit of the park if you wish. Leave the park through Roehampton Gate, skirt Barnes Common and go past the Wetland Centre at Barnes before rejoining the river and following the embankment for a mile or so (1.6km) to the south bank at Putney Bridge.

NEARBY CYCLE ROUTES
The ride described here is the first section of the Thames Valley Cycle Route, which runs from Putney Bridge to Oxford (Route 4 to Reading, then Route 5 from Reading to Oxford). East from Putney Bridge, the Thames Valley Cycle Route runs right through the heart of London to Greenwich and on to Dartford. There is also a traffic-free circular ride around Richmond Park.

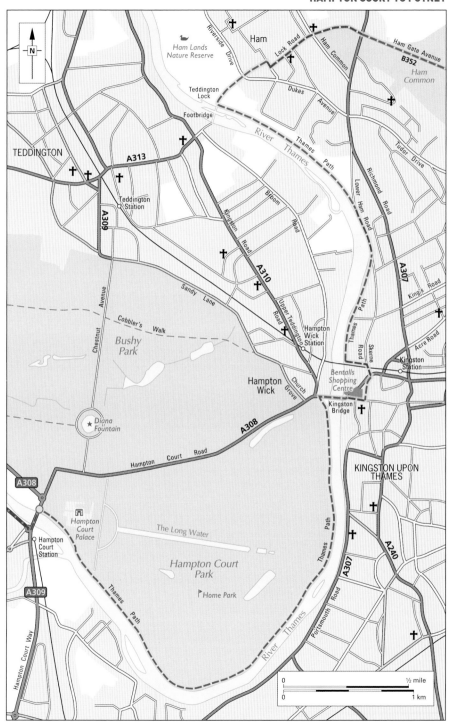

N

Ham Lands
Nature Reserve

Ham

Ham Gate Avenue

B352

Ham
Common

Riverside Drive

Lock Road

Ham Common

Teddington
Lock

Dukes   Avenue

Footbridge

Tudor   Drive

River   Thames

Thames   Path

TEDDINGTON

A313

Bloom

Teddington
Station

A309

Kingston   Road

Lower   Ham   Road

Richmond   Road

A307

King's   Road

Sandy   Lane

A310

Acre   Road

Avenue

Cobbler's   Walk

Road

Upper Teddington

Hampton
Wick
Station

Thames   Path

Skerne

Kingston
Station

Chestnut

*Bushy
Park*

Road

Bentalls
Shopping
Centre

Hampton
Wick

Church   Grove

Diana
Fountain

A308

Kingston
Bridge

Hampton   Court   Road

KINGSTON UPON
THAMES

A308

Hampton
Court
Palace

The Long Water

A307

A240

Hampton
Court
Station

*Hampton Court
Park*

Home Park

Portsmouth   Road

A309

Thames   Path

Hampton Court Way

Thames   Path

River   Thames

0		½ mile
0		1 km

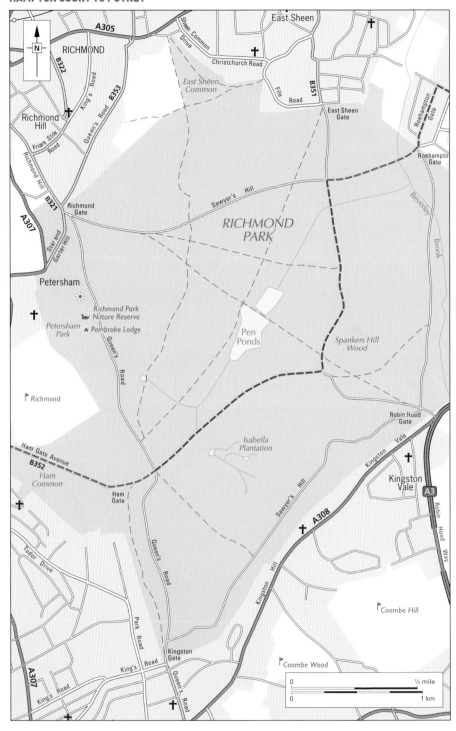

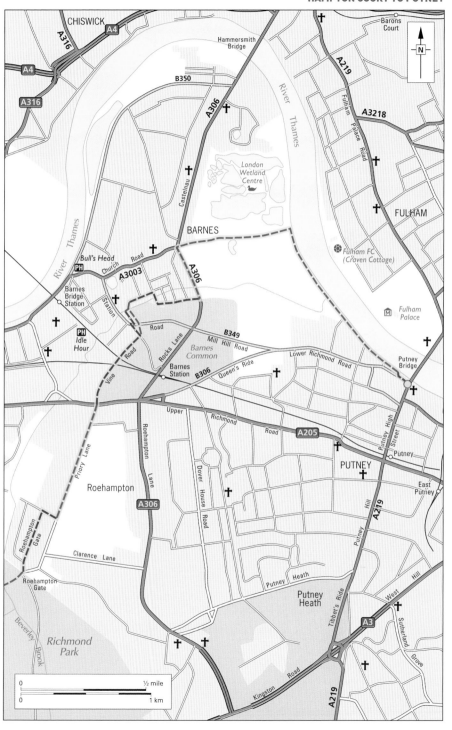

TOWER BRIDGE TO WOOLWICH

This route forms the first part of the Greenway to the Olympic Park at Stratford in east London. It starts below Tower Bridge at the entrance to the Tower of London and follows the remains of the Surrey Canal and Waterways, now known as the Ornamental Canal, through to Shadwell Dock. From there, you can follow a route along the Thames, with wide views over Limehouse Wharf, to Canary Wharf and thence under the Thames through the Greenwich Foot Tunnel. Alternatively, you can go north via Mile End and Victoria Park to the Olympic Park. South of the Greenwich Foot Tunnel, the route connects to the O2 Arena, then winds along the river to the Thames Barrier before cutting inland for a short section to bypass an industrial estate. It then rejoins the riverside leading to Woolwich Ferry for the Royal Arsenal. There are numerous opportunities for return journeys by train, and you can even take a ferry from Royal Arsenal back to Tower Bridge.

ROUTE INFORMATION
National Routes: 1, 4, 13
Start: Tower Bridge.
Finish: Woolwich Arsenal train station.
Distance: 11 miles (17.5km).
Grade: Easy.
Surface: Tarmac throughout.
Hills: None.

YOUNG & INEXPERIENCED CYCLISTS
As much of the route is traffic-free, a one-way trip would be suitable for a family, although care must be taken on the on-road links.

REFRESHMENTS
• Lots of choice all along the ride.

THINGS TO SEE & DO
• Old Royal Naval College: baroque masterpiece on the site of Greenwich Palace, where Henry VIII and Elizabeth I were born; Painted Hall and Chapel open daily; 020 8269 4747; www.oldroyalnavalcollege.org
• National Maritime Museum: one of the greatest maritime museums of the world, containing models, displays, paintings and trophies from every continent; 020 8858 4422; www.rmg.co.uk
• Royal Observatory and Planetarium, Greenwich Park: home of Greenwich Mean Time and the Prime Meridian Line, where visitors can stand in both the eastern and western hemispheres at the same time; 020 8858 4422; www.nmm.ac.uk

TRAIN STATIONS
Numerous, including London Bridge; Greenwich; Woolwich.

BIKE HIRE
• Go Pedal!: delivery to most areas of London; 07850 796320; www.gopedal.co.uk

Antony Gormley's 'Quantum Cloud'

Cars and pedestrians
on Tower Bridge

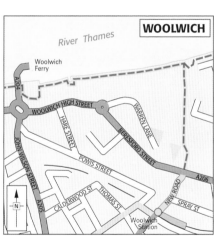

WOOLWICH

River Thames

Woolwich
Ferry

The O2 Arena and
Thames Barrier

- London Tourist Information: 08701 566 366; www.visitlondon.com
- London Travel Information: 0843 222 1234; www.tfl.gov.uk

- On Your Bike, London Bridge: 020 7378 6669; www.onyourbike.com
- City Bike Service: good for exploring the East End of London; 020 7247 4151; www.citybikeservice.co.uk

FURTHER INFORMATION

- To view or print National Cycle Network routes, visit www.sustrans.org.uk
- Maps for this area are available to buy from www.sustransshop.co.uk
- Greenwich Tourist Information: 0870 608 2000; www.visitgreenwich.org.uk

ROUTE DESCRIPTION

Starting from the Tower of London, go under the Guoman hotel on St Katharine's Way, crossing over the Dock Bridge. Shortly afterwards, turn left beside the dock basin, which leads to a zigzag path that drops down under the road. Follow the canalside to the old lock and into Shadwell Lock. Here, turn sharp left to follow round the northern side of the dock, then cross over Glamis Road to reach King Edward Memorial Park on the river frontage. Follow the promenade decking until it runs out in Narrow Street. Continue along

Gate at Old Royal Naval College

Greenwich Park and Royal Observatory

Cycling past the Thames Barrier

Narrow Street until you get close to the entrance to the ornamental gardens, where you turn right under a building and then go across a curved footbridge linking to the promenades running around to Canary Wharf. National Route 1 uses Westferry Road to cross the entrance to the West India Dock before rejoining the riverside. It then winds through residential roads to Mudchute Park and the northern lift shaft to the Greenwich Foot Tunnel. Instead of the lift, you can take the river boat from Canary Wharf to Greenwich Pier.

Follow Route 1, which is signed, through the Old Royal Naval College and then a winding succession of back roads to pick up the Thameside again, just north of Morden Wharf Road. From here, the route follows the Thames Path around the O2 Arena to the

Thames Barrier then goes briefly inland before rejoining the riverside half a mile (0.8km) upstream of the Woolwich Ferry – good for bikes. A little further on you come to the main piazza of the Royal Arsenal site. If you turn away from the river at this point, you cross the main dual carriageway immediately opposite the arched entrance of the Royal Arsenal. Work your way through Beresford Square and the local street markets to reach Woolwich Arsenal station.

NEARBY CYCLE ROUTES

From the *Cutty Sark* in Greenwich, National Route 4 runs along the south side of the river, over the mouth of the Surrey Commercial Docks, to the Kings Stairs and eventually back to Tower Bridge. From here, Route 4 continues west to Bristol and Fishguard. From Limehouse Basin, National Route 1 continues north through the Mile End and Victoria Parks to the Olympic site and the Lee Valley (see page 56). From Woolwich, Route 1 continues into Kent, finishing at Dover.

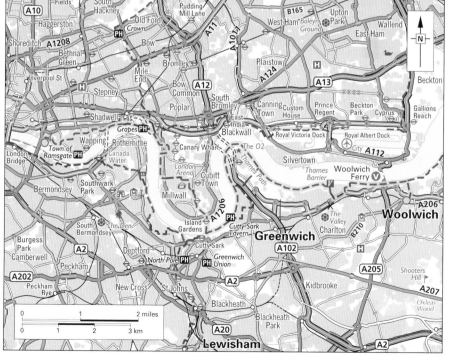

COLNE VALLEY TRAIL & EBURY WAY

This ride gives you a taste of the countryside on London's western edge. It is based around the Grand Union Canal towpath, with options to use the parallel Colne Valley Trail or the Ebury Way railway path from Rickmansworth to Watford. The canal runs close to town centres, the links to public transport are good and the ride is suitable for just about everyone.

The Grand Union Canal runs for 93 miles (150km) from Braunston in Northamptonshire, south through Milton Keynes and the Watford Gap, to join the Thames at Brentford. It took 12 years to build and opened in 1797, when it quickly became a key transport link between Birmingham and London. Many sections of its towpaths are very good for cycling, as you will find on this route – not least because of the numerous pubs and tearooms encountered along the way!

ROUTE INFORMATION

National Route: 61
Start: Uxbridge train station.
Finish: Watford High Street.
Distance: 12 miles (19.5km). Shorter option: from Uxbridge High Street to Rickmansworth High Street 9 miles (14.5km).
Grade: Easy.
Surface: Smooth stone of variable width by the canal and minor tarmac roads.
Hills: The route is mostly flat throughout, except for some steep humpback canal bridges and one hill on the Colne Valley Trail looking over Springwell Lake.

YOUNG & INEXPERIENCED CYCLISTS

The route is suitable for novices and families throughout, although care should be taken along the town centre links.

REFRESHMENTS

- Lots of choice in Uxbridge and Watford.
- Lots of choice along the Grand Union Canal.
- Swan and Bottle pub, Uxbridge.
- Cafe in the Park, Higginson Park, Rickmansworth.

THINGS TO SEE & DO

- The Aquadrome, Rickmansworth: offers a

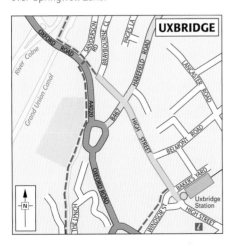

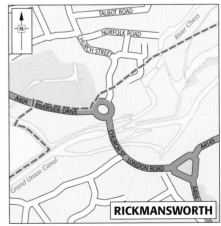

Uxbridge Lock on the Grand Union Canal

wide variety of water-based activities, from fishing to sailing; 01923 776611; www.colnevalleypark.org.uk

- **Colne Valley Regional Park:** farmland and woodland, with 50 miles (80km) of rivers and canals, and over 40 lakes; 01895 833375; www.colnevalleypark.org.uk
- **Batchworth Lock Canal Centre, Rickmansworth:** insight into the past when the River Chess Lock and the Canal Lock

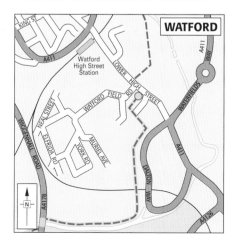

played an important role in travel between London and Birmingham; 01923 778382; www.rwt.org.uk

- **Three Rivers Museum, Rickmansworth:** once Basing House, the home of William Penn, founder of Pennsylvania; 01923 727333; www.trmt.org.uk
- **Croxley Common Moor:** nature reserve beside Ebury Way; www.hertsdirect.org
- **Whippendell Wood, west Watford:** 160 acres of ancient woodland on the outskirts of Watford; used as the backdrop for the ruins of the sacred temple in the Forest of Naboo in the film *Star Wars Episode I.*
- **Watford Museum:** display of various artefacts from prehistory to the 20th century, as well as Watford Football Club memorabilia; 01923 232297; www.watfordmuseum.org.uk

TRAIN STATIONS

Uxbridge (Metropolitan and Piccadilly Lines); Rickmansworth (Metropolitan Line and Chiltern Railways to Marylebone); Watford Junction (for trains to Euston); Watford (Metropolitan Line). Bikes can be taken on most trains out of peak hours.

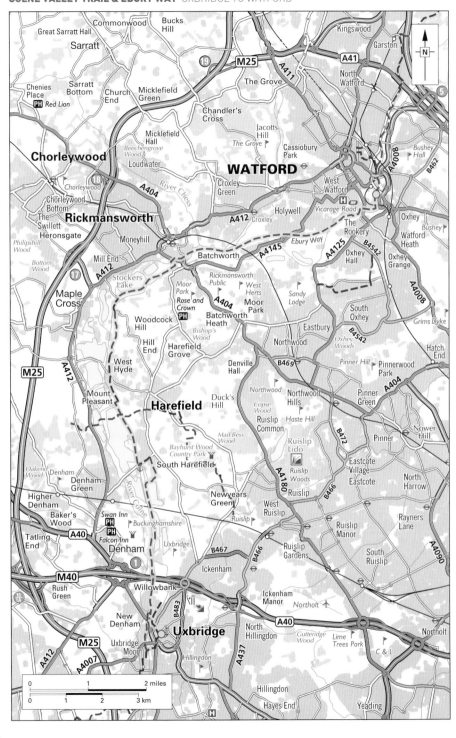

Three Tuns pub at Uxbridge

Canal towpath at Batchworth

BIKE HIRE
Enquire locally.

FURTHER INFORMATION
- To view or print National Cycle Network routes, visit www.sustrans.org.uk
- Maps for this area are available to buy from www.sustransshop.co.uk
- **Grand Union Canal:** 01908 302500; www.waterscape.com
- **Watford Tourist Information:** 01923 226400
- **Uxbridge Tourist Information:** 01895 250706

ROUTE DESCRIPTION
Turn right from Uxbridge train station, through the Pavilions piazza, mix with buses on the High Street, cross over the main road and use the footway to cross the bridge. Turn right onto the canal towpath. This crosses to the east side of the canal just before Uxbridge Lock and then back again before Denham Deep Lock. A little beyond there, cross over a steep humpback bridge marked as the Colne Valley Trail. This takes you along former gravel extraction tracks as far as Widewater Lock, where you must join the towpath again. Cross back over the canal at Black Jack's Lock, then go left to follow Jacks Lane and Summerhouse Lane straight ahead to new housing. Join a woodland path that climbs up for far-flung views over the valley just when you wondered why you had ever left the towpath! A mile (1.6km) after Summerhouse Lane, you have the option of continuing to Rickmansworth town centre, via Riverside Drive and beyond the High Street, to the train station. Alternatively, you can stay on the towpath, going past Batchworth Lock Canal Centre, where you turn left on a couple of narrow bridges to join the Ebury Way to Watford. This woodland railway path crosses the canal a little further on, then continues to Riverside Park. Cross the River Colne via a short section of the main road, turn right by the river and alongside Oxhey Playing Fields to pass under Watford Arches Viaduct for Watford High Street. For a return route, follow this excellent road to the Town Hall and turn west via the roads beside Cassiobury Park to rejoin the Grand Union Canal towpath.

NEARBY CYCLE ROUTES
The Grand Union Canal may be followed to central London. National Route 61 takes you on minor roads to Slough and Windsor in the south, or to St Albans in the north.

LEE VALLEY – GREENWICH TO WALTHAM ABBEY

From the River Thames at East India Dock Basin to Ware in Hertfordshire, the Lee Valley Regional Park stretches 26 miles (42km) along the banks of the River Lee. The 10,000-acre park provides a kaleidoscope of countryside areas, urban green spaces, country parks, nature reserves, waterside trails and the Olympic Park.

The route starts in maritime Greenwich, a World Heritage site, and crosses under the Thames via the Foot Tunnel to the Isle of Dogs, formerly the thriving London dock area. It then takes in many treasures along the way. Beyond East India Dock Road, the Regent's Canal towpath passes through Mile End Park, where a 'green' bridge over busy Mile End Road offers fine views of Canary Wharf. Victoria Park is the oldest municipal park in the world, opened to the public in 1900, while Hackney Marshes have the largest collection of football fields in Europe. The 2012 Olympics inspired an extensive network of greenway routes. Walthamstow Marsh Nature Reserve – a Site of Special Scientific Interest (SSSI) – is one of the last remaining marshes along the River Lee and home to over 300 species of plants. Looking over the river and Springfield Marina is attractive Springfield Park. At Waltham, little is left of Waltham Abbey, but its gatehouse proves its past magnificence.

ROUTE INFORMATION

National Route: 1
Start: Greenwich Foot Tunnel, next to the *Cutty Sark*.
Finish: Waltham Abbey.
Distance: 18 miles (29km).
Grade: Easy.
Surface: Tarmac, grit, gravel.
Hills: None.

YOUNG & INEXPERIENCED CYCLISTS

This route is mainly traffic-free and suitable for young children. Once you join the Regent's Canal, the route is almost entirely traffic-free all the way to the M25.

REFRESHMENTS

- Lots of choice in Greenwich.
- Cafe at Mudchute Farm, Isle of Dogs.
- Cafe in Victoria Park, Hackney.
- Cafe at Springfield Park by Walthamstow Reservoirs.
- Cafe by Stonebridge Lock in Tottenham Marshes.

THINGS TO SEE & DO

- Greenwich Foot Tunnel: www.greenwich.gov.uk
- Museum of London, Docklands: learn about the trading history of the Isle of Dogs and London Docklands; 020 7001 9844; www.museumoflondon.org.uk
- Mudchute Park and Farm, Isle of Dogs: the largest urban farm in Europe; 020 7515 5901; www.mudchute.org
- Mile End Park.
- Victoria Park, Hackney.
- Olympic Park, between Stratford and Hackney Marshes: the route runs adjacent to the park, which is the focus of the London 2012 Olympic Games; www.london2012.com
- Hackney Marshes.
- Walthamstow Marsh Nature Reserve: www.leevalleypark.org.uk
- Springfield Park, Hackney.
- Tottenham Marshes: wide open space, with toilets, canoe and cycle hire and a cafe at Stonebridge Lock; www.leevalleypark.org.uk
- Waltham Abbey Gatehouse and Bridge: 01992 702200; www.english-heritage.org.uk

Office block at Canary Wharf

TRAIN STATIONS
Numerous, including Greenwich; Limehouse; Hackney Wick; Tottenham Hale.

BIKE HIRE
- **Go Pedal!**: delivery to most areas of London; 07850 796320; www.gopedal.co.uk
- **London Bicycle Tour Company, Gabriel's Wharf**: 020 7928 6838; www.londonbicycle.com
- **On Your Bike, London Bridge**: 020 7378 6669; www.onyourbike.com
- **City Bike Service**: good for exploring the East End of London; 020 7247 4151; www.citybikeservice.co.uk

FURTHER INFORMATION
- To view or print National Cycle Network

A cyclist and walkers cross the Lee Valley footbridge

routes, visit www.sustrans.org.uk
- Maps for this area are available to buy from www.sustransshop.co.uk
- **Transport for London Cycle Guides**: free guides covering Greater London, with routes recommended by experienced cyclists; 0843 222 1234; www.tfl.gov.uk/cycling

Ruined gatehouse, Waltham Abbey

Colourful sculpture in Mile End Park

Dogs, home to Canary Wharf and the Mudchute Park and Farm, Europe's largest city farm.

After crossing Millwall Docks and passing the edge of the Canary Wharf development, you join the path of Regent's Canal and Mile End Park, crossing the Mile End Road via a 'green' bridge covered with grass and lined with trees.

Leave Regent's Canal to cross Victoria Park before joining the Lee Navigation canal towards Hackney Marshes. The route continues through Walthamstow Marsh Nature Reserve. North of here, Lee Valley Park has miles of traffic-free cycling, and a route to Waltham Abbey.

NEARBY CYCLE ROUTES

To the east of Greenwich, Route 1 continues along the Thames estuary to Woolwich (see page 48) and then on as far as Gravesend, where it heads inland through Kent, then on to Canterbury and Dover. To the north, Route 1 continues to Roydon and Chelmsford.

Route 21 links London with the south coast via the Waterlink Way, through Deptford and Lewisham towards Croydon and Redhill.

There are also miles of traffic-free cycling in Lee Valley Park, which continues north from the end of the route. The London Cycle Network plus Routes 11, 14 and 54 intersect with the route, providing further on-road options.

- Transport for London Journey Planner: detailed information to help you plan your travel anywhere in Greater London, by bike, on foot or on public transport; 0843 222 1234; www.tfl.gov.uk
- London Cycling Campaign: provides information and advice on cycling in London; 020 7234 9310; www.lcc.org.uk
- London Tourist Information: 08701 566 366; www.visitlondon.com
- Lee Valley Park: 08456 770 600; www.leevalleypark.org.uk

ROUTE DESCRIPTION

Starting in Greenwich, the route takes you under the Thames via the Greenwich Foot Tunnel – please walk your bike through the tunnel. Emerge to find yourself on the Isle of

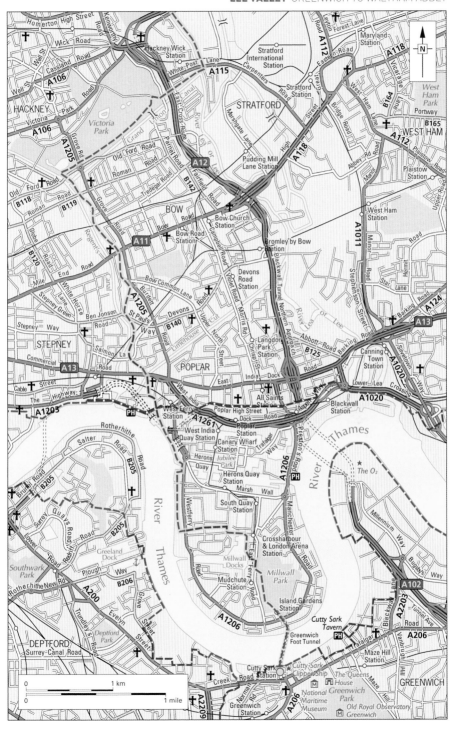

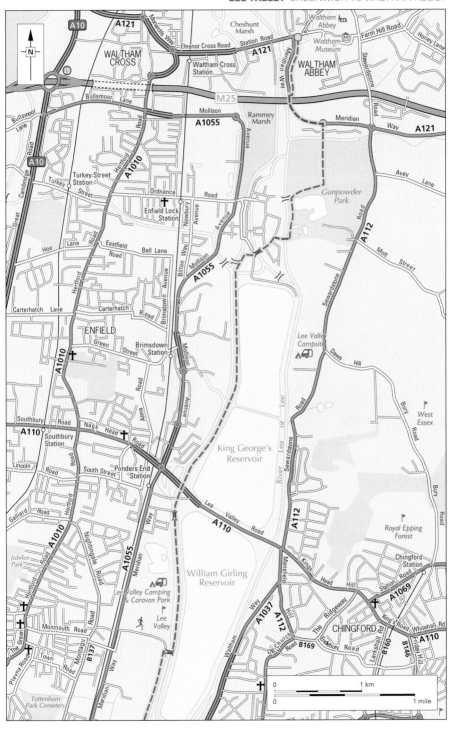

THE BASINGSTOKE CANAL

The Basingstoke Canal runs for some 32 miles (51.5km) from Greywell, near Odiham Castle, to join the River Wey Navigation beneath the M25. This ride is based around the reconstructed towpath that was built as part of Woking's work as a Cycling Demonstration Town (one of 18 towns in England with detailed cycling programmes for 2005–11). The Basingstoke Canal is a perfect place to go on a hot summer's day, as it runs through miles of woods. Opening in 1794, it brought timber from Basingstoke to London, but it was never a commercial success and fell into decline even before the parallel London & South Western Railway opened. Despite years of disuse, it was never formally abandoned, and during World War I the Royal Engineers took over the canal to transport supplies from Woolwich. However, it was abandoned again, becoming derelict. It was not until 1966, when the Surrey & Hampshire Canal Society was formed, that local enthusiasts started a programme that, after 18 years of restoration, led to the reopening of 32 miles (51.5km) of canal in 1991.

Although the core of this ride is the 7 miles (11km) of towpath from Pirbright Bridge to Sheerwater Bridge, pleasant explorations can be made in either direction. To the west, the route runs through Deepcut and past Mytchett Lake, where the Canal Visitor Centre is located, and on through Aldershot and Farnborough, along sections of towpath of varying states of usefulness. To the east, the route joins the Wey Navigation, leading down through Weybridge to join the Thames near the Shepperton Ferry. In Woking itself, there are good links to the town centre, the station and Woking Park, for the remains of Woking Palace. Just to the north of the canal is Horsell Common, the setting for the Martian invasion in *The War of the Worlds* by H. G. Wells.

Monument Bridge near Horsell Common

ROUTE INFORMATION
National Route: 221
Start: Brookwood train station.
Finish: Thames Street, Weybridge.
Distance: 11 miles (17.5km).
Grade: Easy.
Surface: Newly built in Woking, but note that the eastern section, on the Wey Navigation, has a variable-quality towpath, which is perhaps best avoided in wet weather.
Hills: None.

YOUNG & INEXPERIENCED CYCLISTS
The route is traffic-free throughout and very suitable for novices and family riding.

REFRESHMENTS
- Cafe Continental, Woking.
- Ponte Vecchio, West Byfleet.

Autumn colours along the Basingstoke Canal

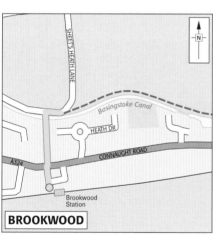

SHEET'S HEATH LANE
Basingstoke Canal
HEATH DR
CONNAUGHT ROAD
A324
Brookwood Station

BROOKWOOD

Ferry
TOWPATH
River Thames
GRENSIDE ROAD
THAMES STREET
PORTMORE PARK ROAD
River Wey
ST ALBANS AVE

WEYBRIDGE

THINGS TO SEE & DO
- **Brookwood Cemetery:** vast, almost rural Victorian cemetery, the largest in the UK; military graves and those of some famous names; guided walks; 01344 891041; www.tbcs.org.uk
- **Basingstoke Canal:** regarded as the richest waterway in England for wildlife; www.basingstoke-canal.co.uk
- **The Lightbox:** centre for art and culture, set up in 1993 by 70 art enthusiasts; 01483 737800; www.thelightbox.org.uk
- **Woking Palace:** remains of a palace built in 1515 by Henry VII on the site of a former manor house; 07722 299026; www.woking-palace.org

TRAIN STATIONS
Brookwood; Woking; West Byfleet.

FURTHER INFORMATION
- To view or print National Cycle Network routes, visit www.sustrans.org.uk
- Maps for this area are available to buy from

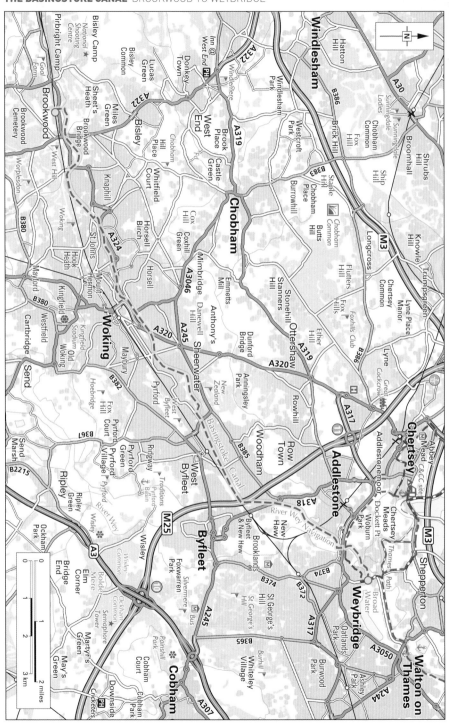

Basingstoke Canal's shady towpath

www.sustransshop.co.uk
- **Woking Borough Council:** 01483 755855; www.woking.gov.uk

ROUTE DESCRIPTION

Starting at Brookwood station, where you will find an entrance to Brookwood Cemetery, cross straight over the main road and join the canal. Turn right along the towpath and continue all the way along the canal to Woking. Almost the only interruption is the first bridge, Brookwood Bridge, where you have to cross the main road as the towpath switches sides. It switches again on the western edge of Woking at Hermitage Road and then again, finally, at Chobham Road by The Lightbox art gallery, museum and cafe. Here, a new toucan crossing will take you straight over Victoria Way into the town centre, where cycling is now allowed throughout the pedestrianized streets. You could follow these through to the station. Continuing now on the south side of the canal, the next bridge you come to, Monument Bridge, is on the southern edge of Horsell Common. Beyond Sheerwater Bridge, the last mile (1.6km) of the towpath remains gravel and you join the Wey Navigation by a footbridge adjacent to the mainline railway. Turn left here and follow the canal northwards on the unsurfaced towpath for about 2 miles

A kingfisher with its catch

(3km) until you come to Weybridge Lock. The Navigation then follows the River Wey itself down to the Thames Lock, where you cross over the footbridge and follow a path through to Thames Street in Weybridge. You could turn left for the Shepperton Ferry and National Route 4 into London. Parts of the River Wey towpath are narrow; care should be used when cycling, and courtesy given to pedestrians and fishermen.

NEARBY CYCLE ROUTES

National Route 4 runs along the Thames from Chertsey and Shepperton Ferry almost all the way to central London, past Hampton Court Palace (see page 38), Kingston upon Thames, Richmond, Kew Gardens, Putney Bridge and Westminster. Local cycle routes are signed through a subway at Woking station.

DOWNS LINK

This route follows the northern part of the Downs Link, which is a largely traffic-free route running from Guildford Castle, set in a gap in the North Downs, all the way through to Bramber Castle, which guards a similar gap in the South Downs. For the most part, the Link follows the line of a former railway, ending at Shoreham-by-Sea. The section described here is extraordinarily rural and takes you through the Low Weald. There is much to see in Guildford itself, including the cathedral, the last to be built in England and consecrated in 1961, and the attractive High Street, sloping down to the River Wey. Once on the route, you cross the Pilgrim's Way, which runs from Winchester to Canterbury along the line of the North Downs, crossing the Wey just below St Catherine's Chapel.

Canal bargeman sculpture, Guildford

ROUTE INFORMATION

National Routes: 22, 222
Start: Town Bridge, Guildford.
Finish: Christ's Hospital train station.
Distance: 18 miles (29km).
Grade: Easy.
Surface: Some sections of the old railway are a little rough but improvements are going on all the time. Except possibly in the depths of the wettest winters, it is suitable for everyone to use.
Hills: The route is almost completely level, except at Baynards Tunnel.

YOUNG & INEXPERIENCED CYCLISTS

The entire route is suitable for novices and families.

REFRESHMENTS

- Lots of choice in Guildford.
- Sandwich bar close to Shalford train station.
- Jolly Farmer pub, near Bramley old train station.
- Numerous places in Cranleigh.
- Red Lyon pub, Slinfold village.

THINGS TO SEE & DO

- Guildford Cathedral: modern cathedral, started in 1933; open to visitors; holds various art exhibitions; 01483 547860; www.guildford-cathedral.org
- Guildford Castle: built shortly after 1066 by William the Conqueror; restored Great Tower; history of the castle to the present

Guildford Castle, in the centre of town

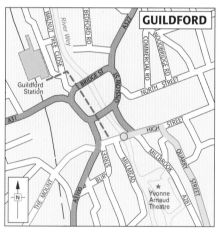

Narrowboat on the River Wey at Guildford

day; 01483 444751; www.guildford.gov.uk
- **Guildford Museum:** founded in 1898, now houses the largest collection of archaeology, local history and needlework in Surrey; 01483 444751; www.guildford.gov.uk

TRAIN STATIONS
Guildford; Shalford; Christ's Hospital.

BIKE HIRE
- **Nirvana Cycles, Westcott:** 01306 740300; www.nirvanacycles.com

FURTHER INFORMATION
- To view or print National Cycle Network routes, visit www.sustrans.org.uk
- Maps for this area are available to buy from www.sustransshop.co.uk
- **Guildford Tourist Information:** 01483 444333; www.visitguildford.com

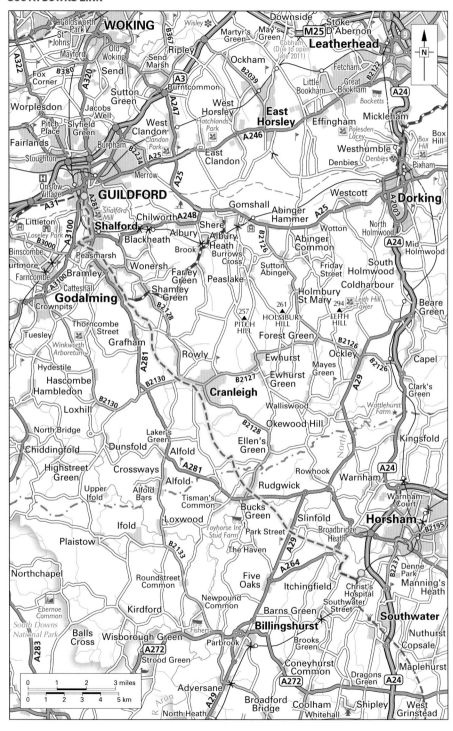

On the Downs Link
near Slinfold

The town **clock** in
Guildford High Street

- Sussex Tourist Information: 01243 263065;
  www.visitsussex.org

ROUTE DESCRIPTION

Starting from the Town Bridge at the bottom of
the High Street, cross at the lights and go up
the street for a few metres before turning right
into Quarry Street, at the end of which you join
the path south across Shalford Park. If you have
come from the station, follow subways under
the road, which lead down to the riverside
(dismount where necessary). After a few twists
and turns, the route eventually crosses over the
railway and leads through to Broadford. Here,
you cross the Wey and pick up a cyclepath on
the north side of the road to join the start of the
railway path under a road bridge.

The railway path then runs past Bramley old
station and takes an uneventful course through
to Cranleigh. For much of this section, the path
runs close to the disused Wey & Arun Canal,
which is planned for restoration and worth
exploring if you have the time. Cranleigh is a
good stopping point, with a number of cafes.
South from here, the route passes through
more and more interesting countryside. At
Baynards, the tunnel is occupied by bats, so
this route doubles back for the only substantial
climb of the trip over the hill above the tunnel.

Beyond Rudgwick, the path crosses the River
Arun on the unusual double bridge, where the
railway inspectors refused to allow the line to
be opened because they considered its
gradients too steep. Instead, they forced the
railway company to build a second bridge above
the first to remedy this situation. Further on,
you may wish to turn left at Slinfold for
refreshments because there is nothing at
Christ's Hospital station.

NEARBY CYCLE ROUTES

National Route 222, the Downs Link, continues
south from Christ's Hospital, while various
segments of the Surrey Cycleway can be picked
up along the route. In Guildford itself, Route 22
runs westwards, to Compton and Puttenham,
and includes an attractive section along the
foot of the Downs, or eastwards towards
Dorking on bridleways and quiet lanes.
Although tempting, the towpath of the Wey
Navigation is not generally a formal cycle route,
except for short sections running northwards
from the town centre.

Just before you cross the main road at
Shalford, there is a local route south to
Godalming, and just after Bramley a new path
to Shamley Green takes Route 22 eastwards to
Shere and, eventually, to Dorking.

WINCHESTER TO ALTON & BASINGSTOKE

This route is a quiet introduction to the beauties of historic Hampshire and the opportunity to follow lightly trafficked lanes through this pleasant county's gently undulating downland, bluebell woods, rolling fields and small villages.

The ride starts in Winchester, the ancient capital of Wessex and a city that should not be hurried through. Winchester Cathedral is one of the largest cathedrals in England, and has the longest nave and overall length of any Gothic cathedral in Europe. The Great Hall of the castle is famous for King Arthur's Round Table, which was painted for Henry VIII with the names of Arthur's legendary knights. The town centre was laid out in a street pattern in Saxon times, overlaying earlier Roman streets. Winchester remained the capital of England until some time after the Norman Conquest in 1066.

The attractive town of New Alresford lies at the end of the Watercress Line steam railway. From Medstead, the main route continues through Chawton Park Wood to Alton, with the option of going north on country lanes to Basingstoke, 28 miles (45km) away.

ROUTE INFORMATION

National Route: 23
Start: Winchester Cathedral.
Finish: Alton train station; Basingstoke train station.
Distance: To Alton 21 miles (34km). To Basingstoke 28 miles (45km). Shorter option, from Medstead to Basingstoke train station 13 miles (21km).

Grade: Moderate.
Surface: Mostly tarmac roads.
Hills: There are some quite long hills, especially up to Medstead, one of the highest villages in the county.

YOUNG & INEXPERIENCED CYCLISTS

This route is not suitable for novices or family groups unless they are used to cycling on country roads.

REFRESHMENTS

• Lots of choice in Winchester, Alton and

Gormley's 'Sound II', Winchester Cathedral

Basingstoke town centres.
- Good selection of restaurants, pubs and cafes in New Alresford.
- The Castle of Comfort pub, Medstead.
- The Yew Tree pub, Lower Wield.
- The Fox pub, Ellisfield.
- The Jolly Farmer pub, Cliddesden village.

THINGS TO SEE & DO
- **Winchester Cathedral:** Romanesque-style cathedral dating from 1079; items of interest include the tomb of Jane Austen; 01962 857200; www.winchester-cathedral.org.uk
- **Winchester Castle:** the magnificent Great Hall is the only remaining part of the 13th-century castle; home of the world-famous medieval Round Table; www.visitwinchester.co.uk
- **The Watercress Line:** catch the steam train all the way to Alton (summers only); 01962 733810; www.watercressline.co.uk
- **Jane Austen's House Museum, Chawton:** Austen's last home before she died and where she wrote *Sense and Sensibility* and *Pride and Prejudice*; 01420 83262; www.jane-austens-house-museum.org.uk
- **War Memorial Park and bandstand, Basingstoke:** historic Georgian park, which hosts many different events; also includes a woodland walk, BMX/skate park and aviary; www.basingstoke.gov.uk

TRAIN STATIONS
Basingstoke; Winchester; Alton.

BIKE HIRE
Enquire locally.

FURTHER INFORMATION
- To view or print National Cycle Network routes, visit www.sustrans.org.uk
- Maps for this area are available to buy from www.sustransshop.co.uk
- Hampshire Tourist Information: www.visit-hampshire.co.uk

Round Table in the Great Hall, Winchester

Jane Austen's house at Chawton

ROUTE DESCRIPTION
Starting from Winchester Cathedral, go towards the river, aiming for the imposing statue of King Alfred the Great, and immediately over the High Street bridge. Then turn left through a cycle gap to a lovely road running beside the River Itchen. There is then a

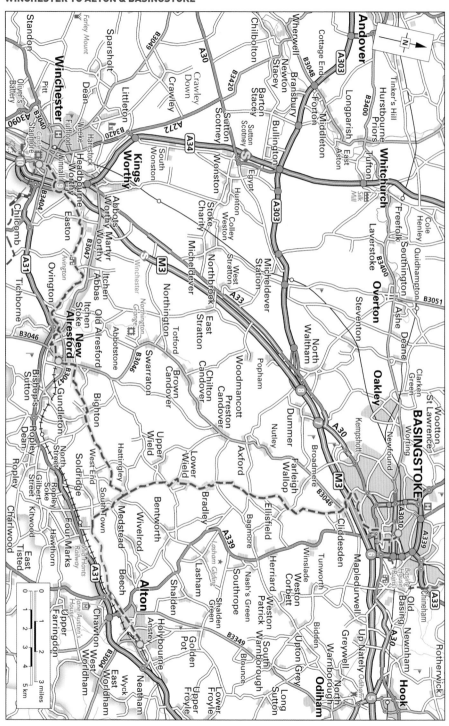

Steam train on the Watercress Line

Old-fashioned sign at Alresford station

Houses in Alresford's East Street

gentle climb up to cross the M3 near Junction 9. Move onto the right-hand side footway just after the first roundabout and then follow the way through two subways to reach a blissful lane to Easton and the gated road through Avington Park – quite beautiful! For the final approach to New Alresford, cross the main road on the cycle track and then turn sharp left after a few hundred yards to wind your way under a railway arch and immediately right to the station and town centre. Note that this first section of the route is not currently signed.

Leaving the town, turn right soon after the Globe pub, past Watercress Farms and Alresford Salads. Continue on this road up to Medstead. Here, there are two options. Either turn right for Alton or left for Basingstoke. For Alton, make sure you go straight on at the next junction across the village green and playing fields. Turn left at the end and go up a short hill into Chawton Park Wood. The entrance is left, just before the car park, but if you miss it, just forage across the grass to the forest track. A couple of miles on, if you want to see Jane Austen's home, turn right down Mounters Lane and go under first a railway bridge and then through the A31 subway. Otherwise, continue straight on for the town centre and Alton station. The Basingstoke option is pretty, with

bluebell woods, wheat fields and good pubs such as The Yew Tree at Lower Wield and The Fox at Ellisfield. The route through Basingstoke takes you through Viables industrial estate, past the offices of various high-tech companies and through the War Memorial Park. Cross London Road and turn right down Eastrop Lane. Route 23 takes you to the right, through Eastrop Park (well worth a visit), but to return to Winchester by train, bear left and follow the signs through a string of narrow subways leading to Basingstoke station, which has frequent trains in all directions.

NEARBY CYCLE ROUTES

National Route 23 continues north from Basingstoke, past the walls of the Roman town of Calleva (Silchester), and north to Reading.

FORDINGBRIDGE TO BROCKENHURST

There are numerous circular rides in the New Forest that are already very popular with cyclists. This ride strings these into a real route and gives you an overall picture of the range of territory secreted away in the New Forest, from the sandy Hampton Ridge, with far-flung views to the north, to deep forests, shallow rivers and open glades to the south. You will be amazed at how many cyclists there are on a fine day in the New Forest. Brockenhurst, with its easy access from London and bike hire shops, is the centre of all this activity. The New Forest, which is a National Park, promotes public access on foot and cycle in consultation with the verderers (official custodians), who have long-standing inherited rights and privileges in the forest. They guard it jealously and have maintained it against many of the ravages of development in the area. They also limit cycling to agreed routes, all of which are described in the Forestry Commission's cycling leaflets.

ROUTE INFORMATION
National Route: Mainly Forestry Commission tracks with a link to National Route 2
Start: The Great Bridge over the River Avon, Fordingbridge.
Finish: Brockenhurst train station.
Distance: Up to 22 miles (35.5km), depending on how many forest roads are incorporated into the ride.
Grade: Medium.

Surface: Gravel tracks on the forest roads.
Hills: Some modest hills.

YOUNG & INEXPERIENCED CYCLISTS
This ride would be good for a novice, but a family group might prefer to tackle some of the forest circuits first, in particular the well-used rides coming out of Brockenhurst. Take great care crossing the A35 before the Rhinefield Ornamental Drive.

Rockford Common

The Foresters Arms at Brockenhurst

REFRESHMENTS
- The Royal Oak pub, near Fritham: homemade bread and pork pies.
- Lots of choice in Lyndhurst and Brockenhurst.
- The Foresters Arms pub, Brockenhurst.

THINGS TO SEE & DO
- **Wild New Forest Ponies:** also keep your eyes peeled for shy roe deer and stags.
- **The New Forest Reptile Centre, near Millyford Bridge:** conservation centre where you can see all of Britain's native reptiles; 01425 476487; www.new-forest-national-park.com
- **The New Forest Centre, Lyndhurst:** information about visiting the Park and New Forest; themed events and exhibitions: 023 8028 3444; www.newforestcentre.org.uk
- **The New Forest Museum, Lyndhurst:** displays and activities relating to the history and geology of the New Forest National Park; 023 8028 3444; www.newforestmuseum.org.uk
- For a list of more attractions in New Forest National Park, visit www.new-forest-national-park.com/new-forest-attractions

TRAIN STATIONS
Brockenhurst.

BIKE HIRE
- **Sandy Balls Cycle Centre, Fordingbridge:** 01425 657707; www.sandyballscyclecentre.co.uk
- **Balmer Lawn Cycle Hire, Brockenhurst:** 01590 623133
- **Country Lanes Cycle Hire, Brockenhurst:** 01590 622627; www.countrylanes.co.uk
- **Cycle Experience, Brockenhurst:** 01590 624204; www.cyclexperience.co.uk

FURTHER INFORMATION
- To view or print National Cycle Network

Blackwater near Rhinefield

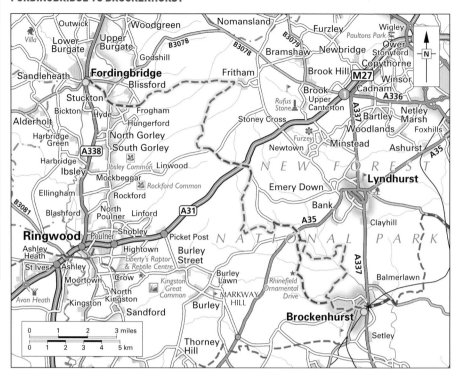

routes, visit www.sustrans.org.uk
- Maps for this area are available to buy from www.sustransshop.co.uk
- New Forest Tourist Information: www.forestry.gov.uk/newforest

ROUTE DESCRIPTION

At the time of publication, this route is not signed National Cycle Network, although some sections have Forestry Commission signs.

Starting from the Great Bridge in Fordingbridge, pass under the A338 main road and, almost immediately, turn right and left for Stuckton and Frogham Hill. Follow the road to Abbotts Well until it turns sharp left, but you go straight on along the gravel road, leading up Hampton Ridge into the open spaces of the New Forest. Follow this eastwards, dipping down to the stream in the Amberwood enclosure until you come to Fritham. Turn sharp right, before you reach the pub, and follow the gravel road southwestwards towards Holly Hatch Cottage. Just past the cottage, turn

left and follow the track up the hill to join the road in the open spaces between enclosures. The first few hundred yards can be busy at rush hour. Go straight over the junction and follow the road through the forest and under the A31.

At the top of the hill, join the Bolderwood Arboretum Ornamental Drive. Take great care crossing the A35. Follow the Rhinefield Ornamental Drive to Brockenhurst, or turn left at the Arboretum for the Pound Hill enclosure and wind your way on gravel roads to a junction. Turn right to the outskirts of Brockenhurst. Skirt around the edge of housing, with the open common on your right, to link through to the town centre and Brockenhurst station.

NEARBY CYCLE ROUTES

National Route 2 along the south coast is signed eastwards to Hythe for the ferry to Southampton, while you can follow minor roads to the west. These will eventually link to Christchurch for the excellent Bournemouth & Poole Promenade route.

COAST TO COAST ACROSS THE ISLE OF WIGHT – COWES TO SANDOWN

Starting in Cowes in the north of the island and finishing in Sandown in the southeast, this might be considered the easiest 'coast-to-coast' ride in the country. Included in the ride are two long sections of railway path. The first starts just south of West Cowes, runs parallel with the River Medina, which is filled with yachts, and finishes on the northern outskirts of Newport. The second, much longer railway path is joined at Shide on the south side of Newport. It takes you through lovely countryside – pasture, woodland and wildflowers – to the outskirts of Sandown, a popular and lively seaside resort with fine sandy beaches.

At 13 x 23 miles (21 x 37km), the Isle of Wight is an ideal size for exploring by bike. It is also blessed with a mild climate, the countryside is largely unspoiled and the local authority has adopted a very positive attitude towards cycling. There are also good transport connections to the English mainland, with ferries sailing from Portsmouth, Southampton and Lymington.

ROUTE INFORMATION
National Route: 23
Start: Chain ferry terminal in West Cowes.
Finish: Sandown train station.
Distance: 16 miles (25.5km).
Grade: Easy.
Surface: A mix of good-quality tarmac roads and tracks, and gravel paths.
Hills: None.

YOUNG & INEXPERIENCED CYCLISTS
The section from south of Cowes to the north of Newport is ideal for families, as is the longer section from the southern edge of Newport to the western edge of Sandown. Care should be taken on the streets in Sandown, Newport and Cowes, particularly on the one-way systems.

REFRESHMENTS
- Lots of choice in Cowes, Newport and Sandown.
- Pointer Inn, just off the route in Newchurch (this involves a steep climb).
- There is often a tea tent at old Merstone train station.

THINGS TO SEE & DO
- Nearly half the island is designated an Area of Outstanding Natural Beauty (www.wightaonb.org.uk). It is one of the few places in England where you can still see red squirrels and Glanville Fritillary butterflies.

Purple flowering garlic

Carisbrooke Castle

Cowes:
- **Osborne House:** Queen Victoria's island retreat; www.english-heritage.org.uk
- **Maritime Museum:** 01983 823433; www.iwight.com

Newport:
- **Remains of a Roman villa:** discovered in 1926 and painstakingly restored; 01983 529720; www.iwight.com
- **Museum of Island History:** 01983 823433; www.iwight.com
- **Quay Arts Centre:** the Island's leading art gallery and venue for live arts events; 01983 822490; www.quayarts.org
- **Classic Boat Museum:** collection of classic boats, tools and other artefacts, with an emphasis on craftsmanship through the generations; 01983 533493; www.classicboatmuseum.org
- **Carisbrooke Castle Museum:** includes local archaeological collections illustrating human settlement on the Island from prehistoric times; 01983 523112; www.carisbrookecastlemuseum.org.uk

- **Carisbrooke Castle, off the route near Newport:** remarkably intact medieval castle with donkey centre and Princess Beatrice Garden; 01983 522107; www.english-heritage.org.uk

Sandown:
- **Dinosaur Isle:** displays of fossils and life-size reconstructions of the Island's dinosaurs; 01983 404344; www.dinosaurisle.com
- **Amazon World Zoo Park, Newchurch, near Sandown:** animal conservation and education centre, with over 200 species; falconry displays and educational talks; 01983 867122; www.amazonworld.co.uk

FERRIES
There are three passenger vehicle ferry routes to and from the mainland, all of which carry bikes free of charge.
- **Southampton to East Cowes:** www.redfunnel. co.uk. (A chain ferry floating bridge connects East Cowes and West Cowes. Bikes and foot passengers travel free of charge; www.iwight.com)

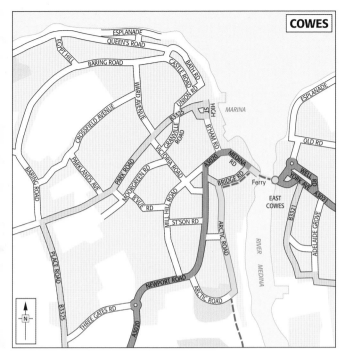

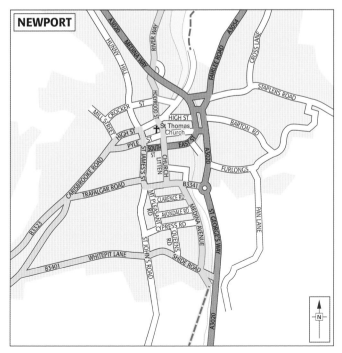

• Portsmouth to Fishbourne: www.wightlink.co.uk
• Lymington to Yarmouth: www.wightlink.co.uk There are also catamaran services for foot passengers running from Southampton to West Cowes (Red Funnel), and from Portsmouth to Ryde Pier Head (Wightlink). Bikes are allowed only on the Portsmouth crossing.

To do this ride in reverse, take the catamaran from Portsmouth Harbour to Ryde Pier Head, and the train connection to Sandown (maximum four bikes); www.wightlink.co.uk for catamaran; www.island-line.co.uk for train link.

TRAIN STATIONS
Portsmouth Harbour; Ryde Pier Head; Sandown.

BIKE HIRE
• Isle of Wight Hire: 01983 299056 (Cowes); 01983 400055 (Sandown); www.isleofwighthire.co.uk
• TAV Cycles, Ryde: 01983 812989: www.tavcycles.co.uk

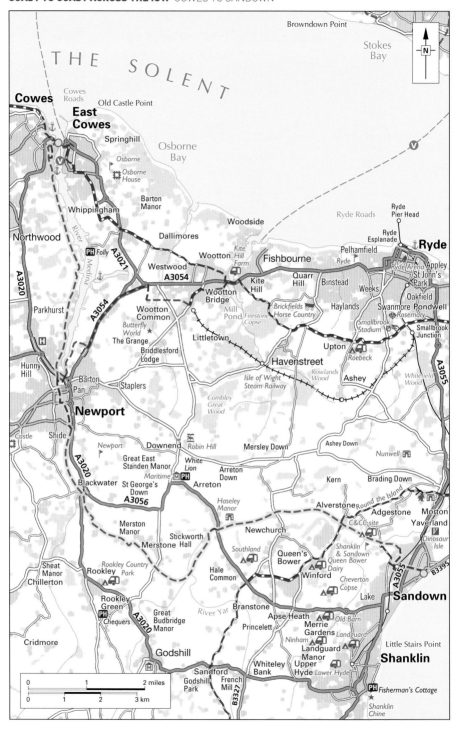

Sandown pier and beach office

You now enter the historic capital of the Island, Newport. After threading your way through the streets and looking out for the route signs, you join the second, much longer railway path at St George's Approach, towards Shide. This takes you through open countryside and a marshland nature reserve, and becomes part of the Sunshine Trail at Merstone.

Continue towards Sandown adjacent to the River Yar via Horringford, Langbridge and Alverstone and go under the railway by Sandown station.

- Wight Cycle Hire: 01983 761800; www.wightcyclehire.co.uk

FURTHER INFORMATION
- To view or print National Cycle Network routes, visit www.sustrans.org.uk
- Maps for this area are available to buy from www.sustransshop.co.uk
- Tourist Information in Cowes, Newport and Sandown: 01983 813813; www.islandbreaks.co.uk
- Island 2000: download the Sunshine Trail map at www.island2000.org.uk

ROUTE DESCRIPTION
From the car ferry terminal in East Cowes, follow signs on your right via Castle Street to the chain ferry to West Cowes. There, follow Route 23 signs from the chain ferry, left into Bridge Road, left into Pelham Road and left again onto Arctic Road to the beginning of the railway path to Newport. The railway path skirts the western banks of the tidal River Medina towards the bustling market town of Newport.

Here, there are wonderful views across the river estuary, with a glimpse of Osborne House on your left. This easy-to-ride tarmac path is well used by walkers and cyclists, and crosses the rebuilt bridge at Dodnor Cottages.

NEARBY CYCLE ROUTES
The Cowes to Sandown route is the southernmost section of National Route 23, which starts in Reading, Berkshire, while Route 22 runs east to west across the island from Ryde to Yarmouth and Freshwater Bay. It is possible to make a circular trip using the Isle of Wight Steam Railway from Wootton to Smallbrook Junction. Cycle from Sandown to Newport, then take Route 22 beside the main road to Wootton and back by steam train.

There are two other short railway paths on the Isle of Wight: Shanklin to Wroxall and Yarmouth to Freshwater Bay. For mountain bikers, there are plenty of fine chalk byways and bridle paths on the western half of the island, including the spectacular Tennyson Trail, with views out to the English Channel and back over the Solent to the mainland. The Round the Island cycle route is a mix of coastal and inland roads and paths.

The Sunshine Trail is a 12-mile (19.5km) circular route from Sandown, via Lake and Shanklin train stations, to the picturesque village of Godshill and on to Merstone, where you join Route 23 back to Sandown.

LANGSTONE HARBOUR

Portsmouth is generally good for cycling. It has always been flat, of course, and the Gosport and Hayling ferries are designed for cyclists, but now with the city's introduction of a 20mph speed restriction throughout, it will become progressively more friendly to cyclists. The Council publishes a number of interesting guides – the Famous Figures Cycle Ride, the Seafront Cycle Route, and this Langstone Harbour Circular, as well as a city-wide cycle map.

The Langstone Harbour Circular is a must-do ride, if only because of the Langstone Ferry, which makes your heart sing when you see the ease with which it caters for cyclists. Much of the circuit is part of the National Cycle Network, including the hard-won cyclepath along the boundary of Farlington Marshes, to bypass the motorway and other main roads separating Portsmouth from Havant.

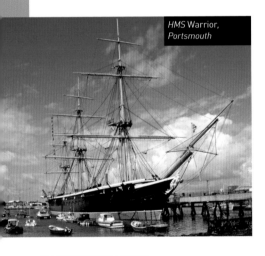

HMS Warrior, Portsmouth

ROUTE INFORMATION
National Routes: 2, 22
Start: Havant train station.
Finish: Havant train station.
Distance: 15 miles (24km).
Grade: Easy.
Surface: Except for the Hayling Billy Trail, which is smooth stone, the rest of the route is tarmac.
Hills: None.

YOUNG & INEXPERIENCED CYCLISTS
Although this route uses some roads, it would make a good introduction for family cycling, especially with so many opportunities to stop off beside the sea.

REFRESHMENTS
- Lots of choice in Portsmouth and Havant, including the Spring Arts and Heritage Centre, Havant.
- Ship Inn by Langstone Bridge.
- Cafe in the Royal Marines Museum, Eastney.
- Ferryboat Inn by the ferry from Eastney.
- Bombay Bay, Southsea Marina.

THINGS TO SEE & DO
- The Spring Arts and Heritage Centre,

Coat of arms on
HMS Victory

Portsmouth's
Spinnaker Tower

Havant: arts centre, with museum and
coastal heritage displays; 023 9247 2700;
www.thespring.co.uk
- Spinnaker Tower, Portsmouth: 170m (558ft)
tall spire with a high-speed internal lift to the
viewing deck, 110m (361ft) up;
023 9285 7520; www.spinnakertower.co.uk
- Charles Dickens' Birthplace Museum,
Portsmouth: re-creation of the Regency
home of Dickens; 023 9282 7261;
www.charlesdickensbirthplace.co.uk
- HMS Warrior: steam and sail ship launched
in 1860; 023 9277 8600; www.hmswarrior.org
- D-Day Museum, Portsmouth: a look at the
largest seaborne invasion ever, which took
place in Normandy on 6 June 1944;
023 9282 7261;
www.ddaymuseum.co.uk

- Ferry trip between Eastney and Hayling
Island: 20–30-minute service; 023 9248 2868;
www.haylingferry.co.uk

TRAIN STATIONS
Havant.

BIKE HIRE
- Cycle World, Portsmouth: 023 9266 6500;
www.cycleworld.co.uk

FURTHER INFORMATION
- To view or print National Cycle Network
routes, visit www.sustrans.org.uk
- Maps for this area are available to buy from
www.sustransshop.co.uk
- Portsmouth Tourist Information:
023 9282 6722; www.visitportsmouth.co.uk

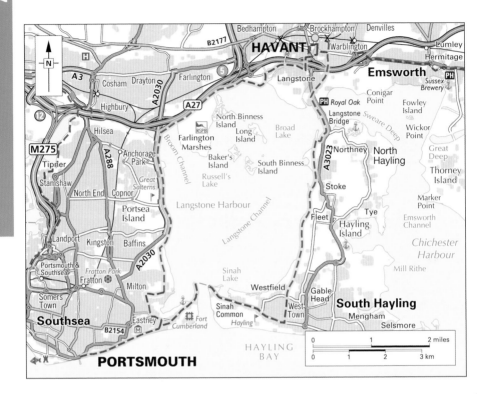

Farlington Marshes

ROUTE DESCRIPTION

Although you can ride this route either way, it is easier to go anticlockwise as you are generally turning left at junctions, and on roadside paths cycling in the same direction as the traffic.

Starting from Havant station, go straight south down North Street to the heart of the old town, over the crossroads, down South Street and first right into The Parchment. You are now following National Route 22. At the end of this, a path takes you to a light-controlled crossing of the main road and into Solent Road, opposite on the right. After a very short distance, turn left beside the stream to pass under the A27. Follow the path westwards beside the road and Langstone Technology Park, to join Brookside and Harts Farm Way. Just before the A27 junction, bear left on the cyclepath, looking out over the water, past Farlington Marshes Nature Reserve and then left beside the Eastern Road, all the time with Langstone Harbour on your left. Just where the road turns away from the sea, peel off onto a gravel path to the University of Portsmouth, then work your way around to the Hayling Ferry, which is specially designed for cycles. To visit Portsmouth seafront join the Esplanade before taking the road to the ferry.

Once on Hayling Island, cycle along Route 2 for a mile (1.6km) or so along Ferry Road before turning left up Station Avenue to join the line of the former railway, the Hayling Billy Trail, which runs close to the harbour towards Havant. Use the western footway on Langstone Harbour Bridge to get back to the railway path.

NEARBY CYCLE ROUTES

The Seafront Cycle Route takes you to the heart of the old docks, the Spinnaker Tower, HMS *Victory*, the *Mary Rose*, HMS *Warrior* and the Royal Naval Museum. Leaflets are available from Portsmouth Tourist Information Centre: 023 9282 6722; www.visitportsmouth.co.uk

National Route 2 runs west via the Gosport Ferry largely to Southampton and east to Chichester (see page 86). Route 22 is intended to go north through the Downs via Rowlands Castle and will eventually be signed to Petersfield and London.

CHICHESTER ROUTES

There can be no more attractive place to start cycling than Chichester. This compact and intimate city has everything you could want for memorable days of cycling: Roman walls, a medieval heart, a magnificent cathedral, Festival Theatre, Fishbourne Roman Palace, nearby beaches, Glorious Goodwood and the South Downs, England's newest National Park. This guide describes just two routes, but between them you can amble from West Wittering Beach to Chichester and West Dean at the foot of the Downs, and link to a number of interesting loops and diversions.

ROUTE INFORMATION
National Route: 2
Regional Route: 88
Start: Tudor Market Cross, Chichester.
Finish: West Dean Church or East Head, West Wittering Beach.
Distance: 6 miles (9.5km) to West Dean. 12 miles (19.5km) to East Head, West Wittering Beach.
Grade: Easy.
Surface: Tarmac and smooth gravel.
Hills: The only hills are short ones approaching West Dean.

YOUNG & INEXPERIENCED CYCLISTS
The Centurion Way railway path to Mid Lavant is particularly suitable for novices and children.

REFRESHMENTS
- Lots of choice in Chichester.
- Ship Inn, Itchenor.
- Old House at Home pub, West Wittering.
- The Beach House restaurant and accommodation, West Wittering.
- Restaurant in West Dean Gardens.

THINGS TO SEE & DO
- **Chichester Cathedral:** dating from 1076 but also famous for its modern art commissioned during the late 20th century; includes a window by Marc Chagall, and a tapestry by John Piper; 01243 782595; www.chicestercathedral.org.uk
- **Chichester District Museum:** exhibitions on local history and artefacts; 01243 784683; www.chichester.gov.uk

CHICHESTER

- **Goodwood:** international sporting venue and home to the Festival of Speed; 01243 755000; www.goodwood.co.uk
- **West Dean Gardens:** features a restored walled kitchen garden, 91m (300ft) long Edwardian pergola, spring garden and beautiful parkland walk; 01243 818210; www.westdean.org.uk
- **Weald & Downland Open Air Museum:** includes 45 original historic buildings set in 45 acres of Sussex downland; shire horses; 01243 811348; www.wealddown.co.uk

TRAIN STATIONS
Chichester.

FERRY
The seasonal Itchenor Ferry runs from the public jetty at Itchenor to the hard at Smugglers Lane, Bosham, linking the footpaths. There is

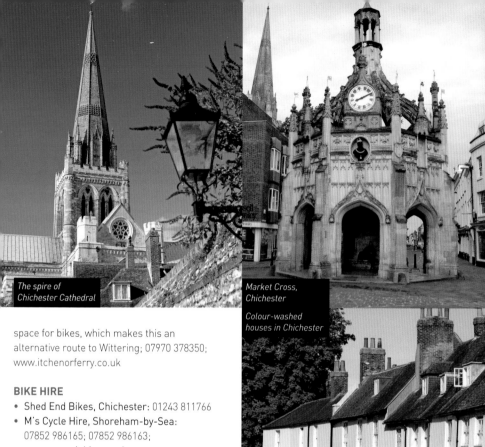

The spire of
Chichester Cathedral

Market Cross,
Chichester

Colour-washed
houses in Chichester

space for bikes, which makes this an
alternative route to Wittering; 07970 378350;
www.itchenorferry.co.uk

BIKE HIRE
- Shed End Bikes, Chichester: 01243 811766
- M's Cycle Hire, Shoreham-by-Sea:
  07852 986165; 07852 986163;
  www.m-cyclehire.co.uk

FURTHER INFORMATION
- To view or print National Cycle Network
  routes, visit www.sustrans.org.uk
- Maps for this area are available to buy from
  www.sustransshop.co.uk
- Cycle Chichester and other leaflets available
  from West Sussex Council on 01243 777610

ROUTE DESCRIPTION
Starting at the Tudor Market Cross in the
plumb centre of Chichester, you can cycle
westwards through the pedestrianized streets
outside peak hours. From the station, go
straight out of the entrance and pick up the
signs towards the cathedral. Just before the
level crossing, turn right onto the railway path,
or if you are going to West Wittering, cross the
railway here. Going north, the route follows the
old railway line – the Centurion Way – which

streams northwards on the western side of
Chichester. After a couple of miles (3km), you
will come to the site of the old gravel pits,
which have been laid out as a shallow
amphitheatre. On the side of the path, exactly
on the line of the old Roman road running north
from Chichester, a squad of Roman navvies
surveys the route – this sculpture made of
scrap metal is by David Kemp, who has done so
much good work for Sustrans. In Mid Lavant,
the railway is subsumed by housing for a short
distance. Then you rejoin it for a mile (1.6km)
before turning left to pick up an attractive path
beside the main road to West Dean, the village
and the church. From here, it is a frustrating
mile (1.6km) of main road to West Dean
Gardens and the Open Air Museum, which is
worth visiting but so difficult to reach.

CHICHESTER ROUTES

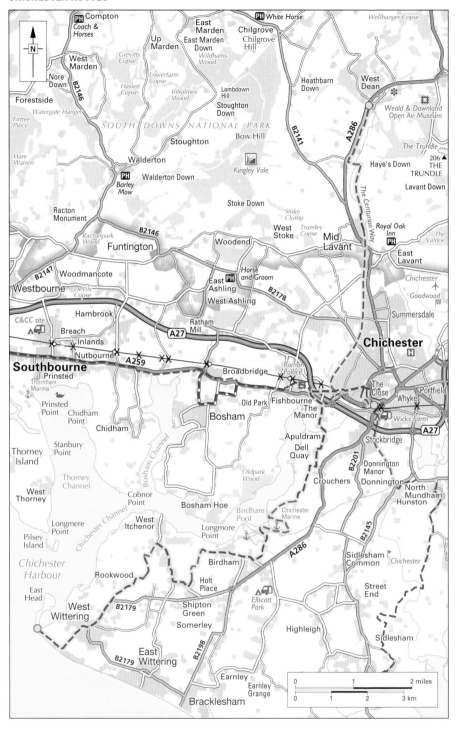

West Wittering's sandy beach

'Chichester Road Gang' by David Kemp

Proceeding south from Chichester, go over the level crossing and follow through under the A27 and then turn left just before the link to Fishbourne Roman Palace (unless you are visiting it, of course), to follow the Salterns Way signs south for the Manhood Peninsular. This route has been promoted by the Chichester Harbour Conservancy, which has done a marvellous job of negotiating attractive paths away from the main road. You eventually reach Chichester Marina, where you can walk over the lock gate or cycle around the dock and then walk over the lock gate of the Chichester Ship Canal, to continue on to Birdham. Here, you turn right to eventually pick up a field path to Shipton Green, then turn right again for 0.75 miles (1.2km) of rather busier road and another section of attractive field path to the outskirts of West Wittering. At this point, you join the local road for just over half a mile (0.8km) before turning off again to West Wittering Beach Park. Go right through this and park at its western end, to walk to East Head and down onto the beach. Note that at low tide, apart from the first 100 yards (100m) or so near the car park entrance, the whole beach through to East Wittering and beyond is hard and makes for a glorious cycle route.

NEARBY CYCLE ROUTES

Your cycling can follow a couple of interesting loops. From East Wittering, minor roads lead through to Regional Route 88 at the Pagham Harbour Information Centre, and back to Chichester. From West Dean, apart from nearly a mile (1.6km) of the busy Midhurst Road, to which no solution has yet been found, you can continue through Singleton, Charlton and East Dean, for Glorious Goodwood and a ride back to East Lavant and Chichester. En route, you will pass the Cass Sculpture Foundation, with its collections set in open woodlands.

Probably the best way up to the South Downs Way is from Charlton, where the road snakes invitingly up a downland valley, or alternatively cross the main road in West Dean and take the lane up to West Dean Woods.

SOUTH COAST PROMENADES – WORTHING TO SALTDEAN

This is probably the best south coast ride in England. Nothing beats bowling along with the wind behind you, the sea glistening on one side and the South Downs occupying the horizon on the other. There is an almost continuous stream of seaside cafes and amusements of every kind. The route is almost completely level, and if the wind is too much, then a train service will take you back again. Note that the promenades can be busy with pedestrians, families and people just enjoying the surroundings, so be prepared to mix in courteously.

ROUTE INFORMATION
National Route: 2
Start: Splash Point, Worthing.
Finish: Saltdean.
Distance: 12 miles (19.5km).
Grade: Easy.
Surface: Tarmac or concrete all the way.
Hills: None.

YOUNG & INEXPERIENCED CYCLISTS
Most of the route is traffic-free, and there are beaches to provide diversions and delays.

REFRESHMENTS
• Lots of choice in Worthing, Shoreham and Brighton.
• Red Lion pub, Hove.

THINGS TO SEE & DO
• **Brooklands Park, Worthing:** miniature railway, playground, cafe and 9-hole par 3 golf courses; www.worthing.gov.uk
• **Brighton Pier:** funfair, amusements and refreshments; 01273 609361; www.brightonpier.co.uk
• **Brighton Museum and Art Gallery:** recent £10 million redevelopment has greatly improved access to the museum's nationally

WORTHING

and locally important collections; 03000 290900; www.brighton-hove-rpml.org.uk
• **Royal Pavilion, Brighton:** opulent seaside palace remodelled in Indian style by John Nash (1815–23) for George, Prince Regent and later George IV; includes historic decorations and furnishings; 03000 290900; www.brighton-hove-rpml.org.uk
• **Brighton Marina:** the biggest complex in Europe; includes a cinema, bowling alley and numerous restaurants and bars; 01273 693636; www.brightonmarina.co.uk
• **Fishing trips:** charter boats from Brighton Marina for groups and individuals; 0800 619 1255; www.seabreeze3.co.uk

TRAIN STATIONS
Worthing; Lancing; Shoreham; Southwick; Hove; Brighton.

Funfair on Brighton's seafront

Shoreham harbour

BRIGHTON (SALTDEAN)

Worthing beach

BIKE HIRE

- **M's Cycle Hire:** delivery and pick-up in the Brighton area; 07852 986165; www.m-cyclehire.co.uk
- **Rayment Cycles, Brighton:** 01273 697617; www.raymentcycles.co.uk
- **Sunrise Cycle Hire, Brighton:** 01273 748881
- **Go Cycle Bike Hire, Brighton Marina Village:** 01273 697104; www.gocyclebikehire.com

FURTHER INFORMATION

- To view or print National Cycle Network routes, visit www.sustrans.org.uk

- Maps for this area are available to buy from www.sustransshop.co.uk
- **Worthing Tourist Information:** 01903 221307; www.visitworthing.co.uk
- **Brighton Tourist Information:** 01273 290337; www.visitbrighton.com

ROUTE DESCRIPTION

While the formal route starts at Splash Point, half a mile (0.8km) east of Worthing Pier, there are plans to allow cycle access on a trial basis to the Promenade as far west as George V Avenue. So it might be best to aim for the Pier, check out the signs, and if the Promenade is open, then enjoy this new facility. The route is continuous, and mostly built on the edge of the shingle, except for a short section of roadside path at Lancing. The new path along the shingle

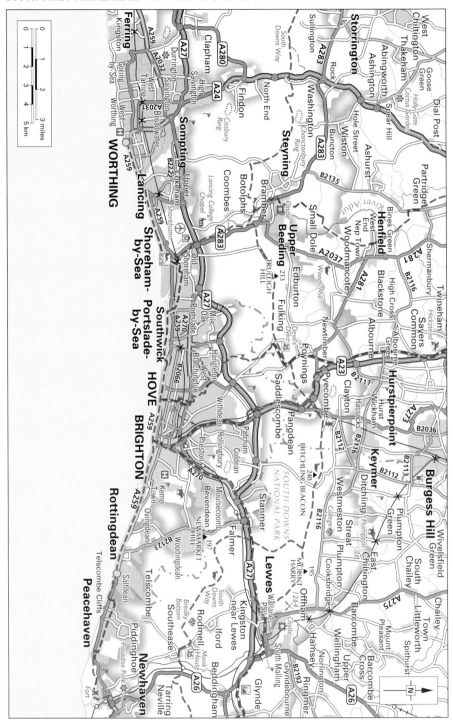

Brighton's Royal Pavilion

spit between the Widewater Lagoon and the sea is particularly memorable.

You then follow the Beach Road before turning left to cross the River Adur on the Drawbridge. At Shoreham the route follows 2 miles (3km) of generally minor roads, first through the town centre past the beautiful 12th-century church of St Mary de Haura, then past the station before eventually passing under the railway by Southwick station. Here, turn left and use the lights to cross the main road to reach the dockside and the path over the lock gates to Shoreham Harbour.

The next mile (1.6km) is a bit industrial, in a marine sense, but at Hove Lagoon the cycling route is again traffic-free to Kingsway, and then again all along the Promenade, past the wreckage of West Pier and past Palace Pier, to Madeira Drive. Here, a new cycle route has been opened beside the Volks electric railway and alongside more beaches. Brighton Marina is another likely diversion and delay to your journey. At this point, the official National Route 2 climbs to run along the clifftop, which is great for views but not as memorable as the Undercliff Walk, which is very well used by cyclists, giving a level route all the way to Saltdean.

Brighton's seafront and promenade

NEARBY CYCLE ROUTES
National Route 222, the Downs Link (see page 66), joins the coastal route at Shoreham. It is best to link to it from the end of the Drawbridge, turn left along High Street and then past the Ropewalk, to join the riverside path under the mainline railway.

At Hove, turn inland up the Grand Avenue Cycle Route, built as part of the Cycling Town demonstration project, and follow Regional Route 82 up to Devil's Dyke and the South Downs Way (see page 94). In Brighton, Route 20 goes through the city centre and up the corridor of the main road to London, which again links to the South Downs Way.

At Saltdean, National Cycle Route 2 continues eastwards to Newhaven and beyond.

HOVE TO DEVIL'S DYKE & LEWES

No section of the South Downs Way is more spectacular than that from Devil's Dyke, past Ditchling Beacon, to Lewes. To get there from the seafront in Hove, a new route has been put together. From Grand Avenue it goes up to Hove Park and then on to join the Dyke Railway Trail, which was opened in 1887 to carry tourists to the beauty spot of Devil's Dyke. The route starts at the beach with the sea at your back and finishes at the historic town of Lewes, guarding the River Ouse gap through the South Downs. All of it is rideable on ordinary bikes, provided you are happy to cope with gravelly surfaces and steep hills, and your pride allows you to walk on occasion!

ROUTE INFORMATION

Regional Route: 82
Start: Hove seafront or Hove train station.
Finish: Lewes train station.
Distance: 17 miles (27.5km). Shorter options: from Hove seafront to Devil's Dyke 5.5 miles (9km); from Devil's Dyke to Lewes town centre 11.5 miles (18.5km).
Grade: The route to Devil's Dyke is quite easy, but the South Downs has some difficult sections.
Surface: Mostly stone and gravel.
Hills: There is a steep climb after King George VI Avenue. The Dyke Railway Trail is easy but the South Downs Way follows with some very steep hills.

YOUNG & INEXPERIENCED CYCLISTS

The route from the Esplanade to Hove Park is built to a high standard and Hove Park has a good circular route within it. There is a difficult crossing of King George VI Avenue (A2038).

REFRESHMENTS

- Lots of choice in Hove and Lewes.
- Plough Inn, Pyecombe.
- Horns Lodge, Lewes.

THINGS TO SEE & DO

- Hove Museum and Art Gallery: features a contemporary craft collection; 03000 290900; www.brighton-hove-rpml.org.uk

The South Downs from Ditchling Beacon

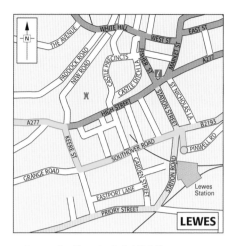

LEWES

- **Pyecombe Church:** delightful Norman church dating back to the 13th century; 01273 857494; www.pyecombe.org.uk
- **Lewes Castle:** Norman origins, with a magnificent 14th-century barbican; 01273 486290; www.sussexpast.co.uk
- **Southover Grange Gardens:** Elizabethan garden, with mature trees, formal borders and lawn for picnics; tea shop; 01273 479565; www.lewes.gov.uk

TRAIN STATIONS
Hove; Lewes.

BIKE HIRE
- Rayment Cycles, Brighton: 01273 697617; www.raymentcycles.co.uk
- Go Cycle Bike Hire, Brighton: 01273 697104; www.gocyclebikehire.com
- Sunrise Cycle Hire, Brighton: 01273 748881

FURTHER INFORMATION
- To view or print National Cycle Network routes, visit www.sustrans.org.uk
- Maps for this area are available to buy from www.sustransshop.co.uk
- South Downs Way: www.nationaltrail.co.uk/southdowns
- Brighton Tourist Information: 01273 290337; www.visitbrighton.com
- City-wide maps of Brighton and Hove are available from Brighton & Hove City Council: 01273 292200

ROUTE DESCRIPTION
Starting at Hove seafront, go straight up the cycle freeway built on Grand Avenue until you

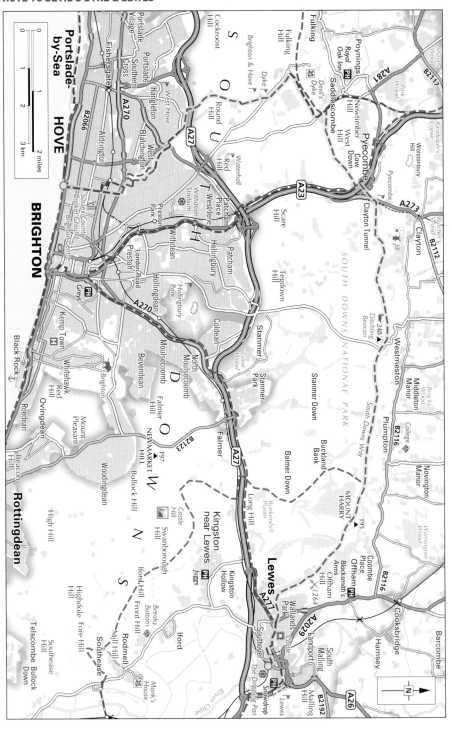

Lewes Castle
gatehouse

View over Lewes
from the castle

Victorian beach huts
on Hove seafront

reach Old Shoreham Road. Cross this
diagonally to pick up the cycle route around the
recreation ground and continue into Hove Park.
If you are starting from Hove station, go out
from the north side, straight up the road
opposite and into the recreation ground to join
the main route. At the top end of the park, go
into Goldstone Crescent, which is an attractive
tree-lined route, leading you to the one difficult
road crossing on this trip. Turn sharp left on
the main road, cross it and walk up a steep
bridleway to Downland Drive. At the end of this,
follow a path around the school and cross the
A27 on a bridge that leads directly to the Dyke
Railway Trail. Follow this for some way, then
continue on minor roads to Devil's Dyke, where
the visitor centre lies in the heart of an ancient
fortification set on an outcrop in the Downs.

If you are continuing, join the South Downs
Way here and travel eastwards to cross down to
the bottom of the hill at Saddlescombe and up
for the first climb of the day. The way drops
down again to cross over the A23 and then
climbs up on the northern edge of the Down,
past Ditchling Beacon. Here, the London to
Brighton Ride comes through and you are
rewarded with miles of open downland. Note
that 2 miles (3km) after Ditchling Beacon, the
South Downs Way turns right, but you must go

straight on past Blackcap and then keep
dropping away on the last few glorious miles to
the top end of Lewes. Just keep going downhill
– don't miss Lewes Castle on your left – until
you arrive in the High Street.

NEARBY CYCLE ROUTES
National Route 2 runs either way along the
seafront to make a magnificent journey through
Brighton (see page 90). The South Downs Way
runs all the way from Winchester to Eastbourne
but you can make a local circuit by turning west
at Devil's Dyke and going about 5 miles (8km) to
join the South Downs Link beside the River
Adur to Shoreham and then back again to Hove.

CHARTHAM TO SANDWICH

Opened in 2011, this delightful riverside path, called the Great Stour Way, provides a safe route into Canterbury and beyond, where you can join quiet country lanes all the way to Sandwich and the Kent coast. The ride starts at Chartham, where paper-making has been a major occupation for the last 625 years. The paper mill dates from the late 18th century. The church of St Mary the Virgin contains the oldest peal of bells in Kent, dating from 1294.

Historic Canterbury's most famous landmark is Canterbury Cathedral, mother church of the Anglican Communion and seat of the Archbishop of Canterbury. Founded in 597 AD by Emperor Augustine, it forms a World Heritage Site along with the Saxon St Martin's Church and St Augustine's Abbey. The city is a haven for cycling and the Tour de France has visited twice, in 1994 and in 2007, when it hosted the finish for Stage 1. From Canterbury the ride is mostly traffic-free to Fordwich where it joins quiet country lanes to Sandwich.

ROUTE INFORMATION

Start: Chartham train station.
Finish: The Guildhall, Sandwich.
Distance: 15 miles (24km).
Grade: Easy.
Surface: A mixture of well-surfaced paths and quiet country lanes.
Hills: There is one steep hill outside Fordwich but otherwise the route is mostly flat.

YOUNG & INEXPERIENCED CYCLISTS

The Great Stour Way from Chartham to Canterbury is completely traffic-free and is ideal for young and inexperienced cyclists.

Boating on the River Stour

Through Canterbury the route is well signed and avoids the busiest roads but it is shared with traffic so may not suit riders of all abilities. Beyond the city centre the route becomes traffic-free again before joining quiet lanes to Sandwich.

REFRESHMENTS

- Lots of choice in Canterbury.
- Salutation tearoom, Sandwich.
- The famous Red Lion pub, Stodmarsh.
- Fordwich Arms.
- George and Dragon pub, Fordwich.

THINGS TO SEE & DO

- **Secret Gardens, Sandwich:** beautiful gardens enclosed by old city walls; 01304 619919; www.the-secretgardens.co.uk
- **Richborough Roman Fort & Ampitheatre:** important Roman site on Kent marshes; 01304 612013; www.english-heritage.org.uk
- **Canterbury Cathedral:** Mother Church of the Anglican Communion; www.canterbury-cathedral.org
- **Marlowe Theatre, Canterbury:** 01227 787787 www.marlowetheatre.com
- **Roman Museum, Canterbury:** 01227 785575; www.canterbury.co.uk
- **Canterbury Castle:** begun by William the Conqueror around 1070; 01227 378 100; www.canterbury.co.uk

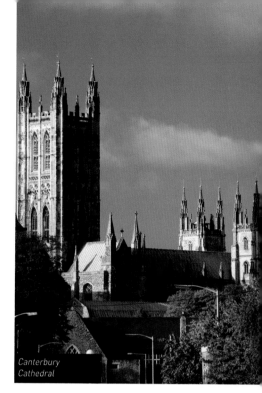
Canterbury Cathedral

TRAIN STATIONS
Chartham; Canterbury West; Sandwich.

BIKE HIRE
- Downland Cycles: 01227 479643;
  www.downlandcycles.co.uk
- Canterbury Cycle Hire: 07791 114529;
  www.wcch.co.uk

FURTHER INFORMATION
- To view or print National Cycle Network
  routes, visit www.sustrans.org.uk
- Maps for this area are available to buy from
  www.sustransshop.co.uk
- Canterbury Visitor Centre: 01227 378100;
  www.canterbury.co.uk/

ROUTE DESCRIPTION
Starting on Rattington Street in the centre of
Chartham village, follow the signs for National
Cycle Network (NCN) Route 18 along the Great
Stour Way alongside the river towards
Canterbury. Follow the traffic-free route for the
next 3 miles (5km) until you reach Whitehall
Road car park. Turn right onto Whitehall Road
following the NCN18 signs under the A2050.
Turn right onto Whitehall Bridge Road following
the signs which now read NCN1. Cross the
River Stour outside the Guildhall and follow
NCN1 signs left into Pound Lane alongside the
river. Turn right at the T-junction with
Northgate and second right into New
Ruttington Lane. Cross Military Road into Old
Ruttington Lane to join the NCN1 traffic-free
path avoiding the A28. Re-join Military Road
briefly before the route becomes traffic-free
again next to the sports centre. Here you are on
the Dover to Whitstable bridleway, signed as
NCN1, all the way to Fordwich. At Fordwich
Road turn right next to the George and Dragon
pub car park. Turn right on to High Street,
which becomes Well Lane, and then follow the
NCN1 signs on quiet lanes on to Stodmarsh
Road. Follow the NCN1 signs all the way
through the villages of Stodmarsh, Preston,
Elmstone, Upper and Lower Goldstone and
Richborough, where you will see the Roman
Fort and Amphitheatre. Continue along
Richborough Road under the A256 and then
turn left into Ash Road, which takes you into the
centre of Sandwich.

NEARBY CYCLE ROUTES
Kent is rich in attractive, safe and enjoyable
cycle routes, and these include:
- The Heron Trail from Higham to Upnor
  on the Hoo Peninsular following Regional
  Route 18.
- The Coast to Cathedral (Dover to Canterbury)
  route following Regional Routes 16 and 17.
- The Crab and Winkle Way from Canterbury to
  Whitstable following NCN1.
- The Viking Coastal Trail from Sandwich to
  Reculver on Regional Route 15.
- Tonbridge Castle to Penshurst Place
  following Regional Route 12.
- Sandwich in Kent to Rye in East Sussex on
  NCN Routes 1 and 2.
- Ashford to Tunbridge Wells following NCN18.

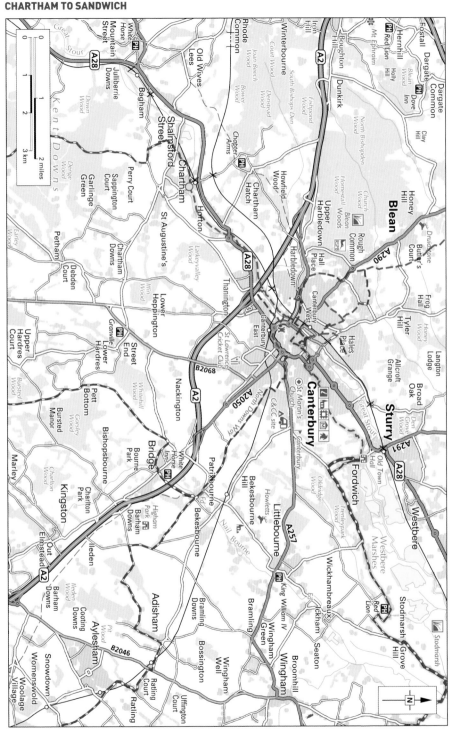

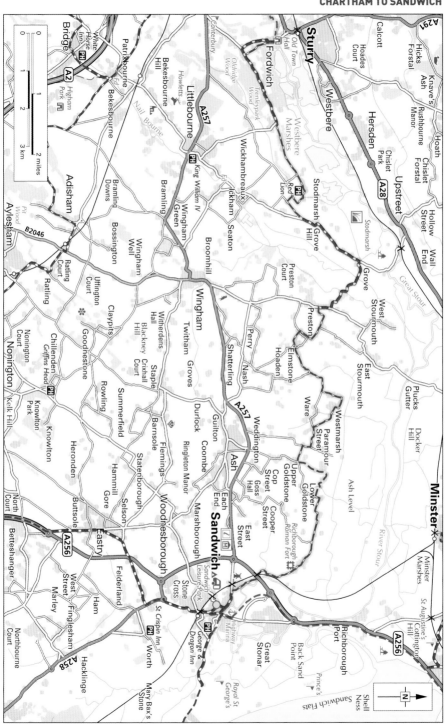

HEVER TO TONBRIDGE

Although this route is only 14 miles (22.5km) in length, you can scarcely do it justice in a single day. Edenbridge is a most attractive town, surrounded by an area full of fascinating places. Nearby lies Hever Castle, where Henry VIII wooed Anne Boleyn, the mother of Elizabeth I. You could spend a whole day at Hever but then, just a few miles on, there is Chiddingstone Castle, with varied collections of Japanese armour and Buddhist artefacts. The nearby village of Chiddingstone, owned by the National Trust, has a row of timber houses, a village shop and a lovely church, as well as the Castle Inn, which shouldn't be missed.

Lunch here, though, can be a protracted affair, which will hardly put you in good shape for the next few miles of cycling to Penshurst Place. This manor house, said to be the finest and most complete example in England of 14th-century domestic architecture, also demands an extensive visit. From Penshurst Place, all you then have to do is cycle the beautiful route to Tonbridge, which boasts what is reputedly England's finest example of a motte-and-bailey castle, strategically positioned above the River Medway.

ROUTE INFORMATION
Regional Route: 12
Start: Edenbridge Town train station.
Finish: Tonbridge Castle.
Distance: 14 miles (22.5km). Shorter option: from Hever train station to Tonbridge Castle 11 miles (17.5km).
Grade: Medium.
Surface: Gravel links.
Hills: There are some hills between Hever and Penshurst.

YOUNG & INEXPERIENCED CYCLISTS
Families will find the 5-mile (8km) journey between Penshurst and Tonbridge a delight, with only one hill up to Well Places Farm. The climb is rewarded with a panoramic view to the west looking out to Penshurst Place. The remainder of the route follows minor roads, so a little more confidence is required.

REFRESHMENTS
- Lots of choice in Edenbridge and Tonbridge.
- King Henry VIII pub, Hever.
- Castle Inn, Chiddingstone.
- Two tearooms and the Leicester Arms, Penshurst.
- Cafe at Penshurst Place.

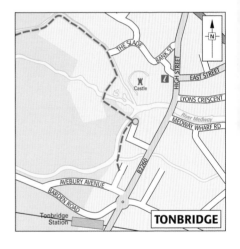

THINGS TO SEE & DO
- **Eden Valley Museum, Edenbridge:** promotes research into the history of the Eden Valley; includes various displays of local history: 01732 868102; www.evmt.org.uk
- **Hever Castle & Gardens:** dating from 1270 and once home to Anne Boleyn; includes a water maze and gardens; 01732 865224; www.hevercastle.co.uk
- **Chiddingstone Castle:** well-maintained castle, dating back to 1500; home to

Hever Castle, home of Anne Boleyn

collections including Egyptian and Buddhist artefacts and Japanese armour; 01892 870347; www.chiddingstonecastle.org.uk
- **Penshurst Place:** 14th-century manor house and eye-catching garden; includes tapestries, paintings and furniture dating back to the 15th, 16th and 17th centuries; 01892 870307; www.penshurstplace.com
- **Tonbridge Castle:** 11th-century castle, with one of the country's finest examples of a motte-and-bailey gatehouse; 01732 770929; www.tonbridgecastle.org

Chiddingstone Castle

TRAIN STATIONS
Edenbridge Town; Hever; Tonbridge.

(If you are returning by train from Tonbridge, you will arrive at Edenbridge station, which is about half a mile (0.8km) north of the town centre and on a different railway line from Edenbridge Town station!)

BIKE HIRE
- **Cycle-Ops, Tonbridge:** 01732 500533; www.cycle-ops.co.uk

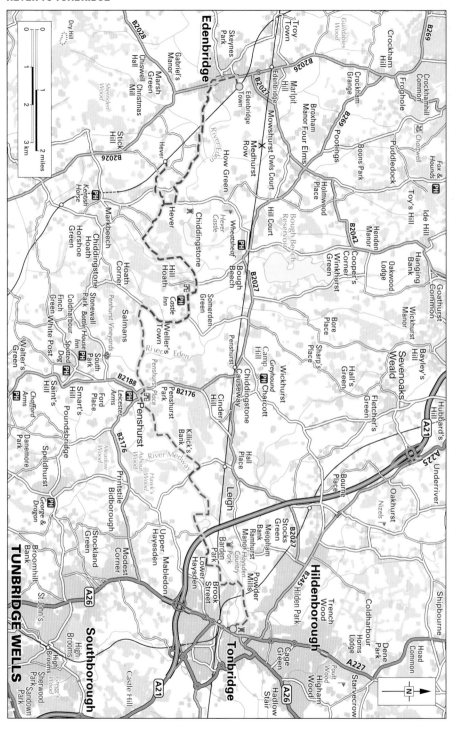

A riot of colour at Tonbridge Castle

FURTHER INFORMATION

- To view or print National Cycle Network routes, visit www.sustrans.org.uk
- Maps for this area are available to buy from www.sustransshop.co.uk
- Heart of Kent Tourist Information: www.visitheartofkent.com

ROUTE DESCRIPTION

Starting from Edenbridge Town station, turn left down the bypassed High Street, passing the Eden Valley Museum on your right. Just south of the roundabout, turn left onto Hever Road. The route to Hever Castle is well signed, but if you want to avoid this road, then take the train to Hever train station, turn right on exiting and then left and right across the main road in Hever. Just over the top of the hill, turn left onto a path at the edge of the wood, which runs level with Hever Church and the castle entrance. Retrace your steps along the path by the woods, turn left and follow the minor roads up and down hills, turning left at each junction, to Chiddingstone Castle – the entrance is just before the village. You can walk past the castle and across the lake to reach the Castle Inn. Sometime later, no doubt, continue on this road, turn right to Wellers Town and half a mile (0.8km) beyond this hamlet near the top of the

Riding away from Penshurst Place

hill turn left. At Wat Stock Farm, be careful to continue left along the green lane, which can be fairly muddy, down to Penshurst. In the village, go straight through the archway to Penshurst Place. The route climbs up to Well Place for a magnificent section of estate road, with wide views towards Tonbridge and the Medway Valley. Eventually, you pass under the A21 and turn left into Haysden Country Park, passing twice under railways, winding beside rivers and ending up at the leisure centre car park and Tonbridge Castle. The train station is at the south end of the High Street.

NEARBY CYCLE ROUTES

Route 21 goes from London via East Grinstead to the South Coast. Route 18 goes from Tunbridge Wells to Ashford.

RYE TO LYDD

Romney Marsh is a natural magnet for the idle cyclist because it is flat – dead flat, and crossed by a tantalizing network of minor roads, their only fault being that they don't conveniently link all the way through to the main towns on the edge of the marsh. This route picks up newly built routes designed to avoid the main traffic from Rye to Camber, and continues to Lydd, with its high church tower know locally as the 'Cathedral of the Marsh'. From here, you can follow the quietest of roads to Old Romney, St Mary in the Marsh and on to the sea wall at Dymchurch for a spectacular ride towards Hythe. Alternatively, follow the road from Lydd, through the shingle banks to Dungeness, and pick up the Romney, Hythe & Dymchurch Railway to take you further up the coast. Rye, like New Romney and Hythe, is one of the Cinque Ports. These towns received royal charters granting rights and privileges in return for supplying ships to the Crown to defend the vulnerable Sussex and Kent coasts. It is hard to think that the small town of Rye was once at the heart of England's defences against its enemies in Europe. At the other end of the ride, Lydd is an equally ancient town, with a church and museum that are well worth a visit. In between lies Camber Sands, the place to stop by the sea with its miles of sandy beaches.

ROUTE INFORMATION

National Route: 2
Start: Rye train station.
Finish: St Mary's Church, Lydd.
Distance: 9 miles (14.5km).
Grade: Easy.
Surface: Good, although from Jury's Gap at the end of Camber Sands the path follows a gravel surface to Lydd, avoiding the parallel tarmac road, which is only busy at certain times of day.
Hills: The route is essentially flat.

YOUNG & INEXPERIENCED CYCLISTS

Largely traffic-free, except through Camber.

Sand dunes at
Camber Sands

Rye Windmill on the River Tillingham

REFRESHMENTS

Numerous cafes and pubs in Rye and Lydd, including:
- The George in Rye.
- The Mermaid Inn, Rye.
- Rye River Cafe, Rye.
- The Star Inn, Lydd.

THINGS TO SEE & DO

- **Rye Castle Museum, Rye:** insight into the medieval history of Rye dating back to the 13th century; includes a history of Rye Harbour and the Ypres Tower; 01797 226728; www.ryemuseum.co.uk
- **Rye Farmers' Market:** weekly Wednesday market with the finest offerings from East Sussex farmers; 01797 280282; www.ryemarket.org.uk
- **All Saints Church, Lydd:** one of the biggest churches in Kent, known as the 'Cathedral of the Marsh'; parts date from AD 740; 01797 320108; www.parishoflydd.co.uk
- **Lydd Town Museum, Lydd:** exhibitions relating to the local area; includes large machinery and vehicles; 01797 366566; www.lyddtownmuseum.co.uk
- **Dungeness Bird Observatory:** excellent bird-watching; 01797 321309; www.dungenessbirdobs.org.uk

TRAIN STATIONS

Rye.

BIKE HIRE

- **Rye Hire, Rye:** 01797 223033
- **Romney Cycles, New Romney:** 01797 362155; www.romneycycles.co.uk

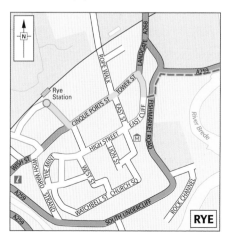

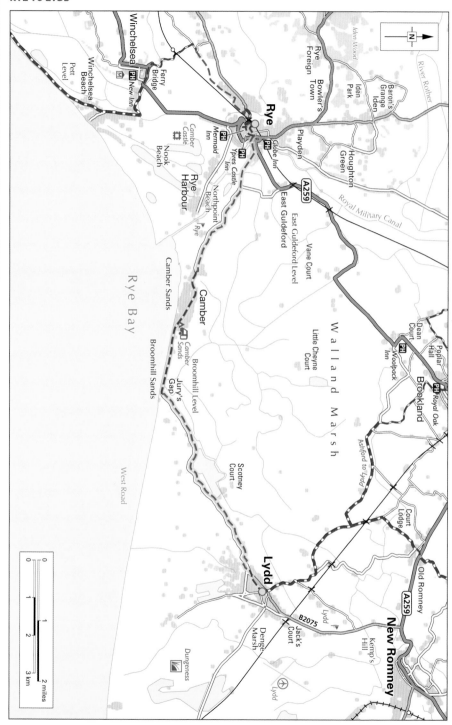

Boats in the harbour at Rye

The beach at Camber Sands

FURTHER INFORMATION

- To view or print National Cycle Network routes, visit www.sustrans.org.uk
- Maps for this area are available to buy from www.sustransshop.co.uk
- Rye Tourist Information: www.visitrye.co.uk

ROUTE DESCRIPTION

Leaving Rye train station, turn left and follow the road round in the Lydd direction before doubling back under Landgate Tower. Then join the steep shared-use path down to the A259 and Lucknow Place car park (the best place to park if you arrive by car). Just after crossing the River Rother, turn right on a traffic-free path to Camber. The River Rother itself is most interesting: in the Great Storm of 1287, the river changed its course from flowing east past Lydd and New Romney to flowing south past Rye. In the process, the original ports of Lydd and New Romney were silted up and lost. In Camber, the Old Lydd Road takes you closer to the sea, and various paths can keep you away from the main road through the village for some of the way, but eventually you will have to rejoin the Lydd road as far as Jury's Gap for a traffic-free path through to Lydd. On the right are military firing ranges, on the left are the endless expanses of the marshes.

NEARBY CYCLE ROUTES

From Rye, National Route 2 continues westwards to Winchelsea for signposted routes through to Hastings. To the east, Route 2 continues through to Hythe and Dover, with links north to Ashford.

THE CUCKOO TRAIL

The Cuckoo Trail is one of the longest and most popular railway paths in the southeast of England. According to Sussex tradition, the first cuckoo of the year was released from a cage every spring at Heathfield Fair, hence the name Cuckoo Line given to the original railway line. The trail offers superb traffic-free cycling through a mixture of broad-leaved woodland, open grassland, arable farmland and pasture. There is a gentle 122m (400ft) climb up from Polegate to Heathfield, so that you can look forward to a gravity-assisted return journey!

As you head back down towards Polegate, you can see the rolling chalk hills of the South Downs ahead of you. There are lots of sights, sounds and smells to experience along the way: metal sculptures, an arch in the form of a Chinese pagoda roof, a claw-like hand and plenty of carved wooden seats with a variety of motifs, made from local oaks blown down in the Great Storm of 1987. In May, look out for butterflies such as the orange-tip. You might even see bullfinch, lesser whitethroat, cuckoos and weasels. There's also pungent wild garlic growing at several places between Hellingly and Horam, and, in early summer, you might come across orchids near path edges and under trees.

The route can be followed in either direction, but the climb from Polegate to Heathfield makes it easier heading south than north!

ROUTE INFORMATION
National Route: 21
Start: Either Eastbourne seafront, near Sovereign Leisure Centre, 1 mile (1.6km) east of the Pier; or Hampden Park train station, 2 miles (3km) north of Eastbourne town centre; or Polegate train station, centre of Polegate village, 4 miles (6.5km) north of Eastbourne.
Finish: Heathfield.

Distance: 16 miles (25.5km) from Eastbourne seafront to Heathfield; 13 miles (21km) from Hampden Park train station; and 11 miles (17.5km) from Polegate train station.
Grade: Easy.
Surface: Tarmac roads and fine gravel paths.
Hills: There is a gentle climb over 11 miles (17.5km) from Polegate up to Heathfield, and there are two short climbs that take you over

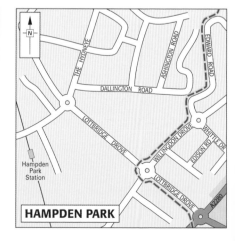

SOVEREIGN MARINA

HAMPDEN PARK

Cattle Creep Bridge
by Eric Lamprell

bridges across the railway and the A27.

YOUNG & INEXPERIENCED CYCLISTS

The link from Eastbourne seafront to Hampden Park is not suitable for very young children so we advise young families to start from Hampden Park or Polegate, where the traffic-free Cuckoo Trail begins.

REFRESHMENTS

- Lots of choice at Sovereign Harbour.
- Various options in Hampden Park, Polegate, Hailsham and Heathfield.

- Tearooms on the trail at the Old Loom Mill Craft Centre (2 miles/3km north of Polegate, just before crossing the B2104).
- Cafe in Horam.

THINGS TO SEE & DO

- **Sovereign Harbour, east of Eastbourne:** one of the largest marinas in the UK, with five separate harbours, and restaurants and shops overlooking the water.
- **Sussex Farm Museum, Horam:** 01435 813352; www.sussexmuseums.co.uk
- **Pevensey Castle, just off the route:** a history

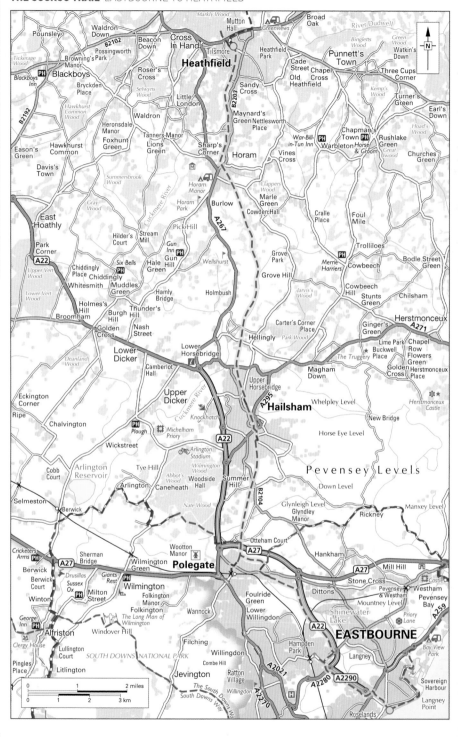

Formal gardens at Eastbourne

stretching back over 16 centuries; www.english-heritage.org.uk
- **Shinewater Country Park:** Eastbourne's newest park, with landscaping completed as part of the Golden Jubilee Way; www.eastsussex.gov.uk/leisureandtourism
- Metal sculptures by local artist Hamish Black. Carved wooden seats, made from local oaks blown down in the Great Storm of 1987, by the sculptor Steve Geliot.
- Victorian brick arch bridges between Hellingly and Horam.

TRAIN STATIONS
Hampden Park; Polegate.

BIKE HIRE
- **Cycleman, Eastbourne:** 01323 501157
- **M's Cycle Hire:** five or more bikes, delivered and collected; www.m-cyclehire.co.uk

FURTHER INFORMATION
- To view or print National Cycle Network routes, visit www.sustrans.org.uk
- Maps for this area are available to buy from www.sustransshop.co.uk
- **Sussex Tourist Information:** 01243 263065; www.visitsussex.org
- **Eastbourne Tourist Information:** 0871 663 0031; www.visiteastbourne.com

ROUTE DESCRIPTION
From Eastbourne seafront, near Sovereign Leisure Centre, 1 mile (1.6km) east of the pier, take the traffic-free path on the west side of Lottbridge Drove. Follow this all the way through the built-up area, across the A2280 roundabout to the next roundabout, where you take the right-hand turn onto Willingdon Drove. (Hampden Park is just a stone's throw from here: carry on up Lottbridge Drove to the next roundabout and turn left on Mountfield Road.) From Willingdon Drove, look out for Edward Road on the left at the next roundabout. This will lead you into Shinewater Country Park, where after a left and a right turn, you reach a bridge. This will take you to Route 21, which is signed all the way to Polegate.

Between Polegate and Heathfield, the route follows the old railway line with a very gentle climb. Where bridges have been dismantled and houses built on the old line, the route continues on short sections of estate roads through Hailsham and Horam, rejoining the railway path, which continues to Heathfield. Where width allows, there's a parallel bridle path, picnic tables and cycle parking hoops.

NEARBY CYCLE ROUTES
The Cuckoo Trail is part of National Route 21, which runs south from London through Redhill and East Grinstead to Eastbourne. From Polegate, the South Coast Cycle Route (Route 2) runs east through Pevensey to Bexhill and west to Newhaven and Brighton. The Forest Way and Worth Way railway paths start in East Grinstead, running west to Crawley and east to Groombridge. Eastbourne, Hastings, Brighton and Hove Promenades have cycle tracks (see page 90). The South Downs Way is good for fit cyclists on mountain bikes (see page 94). There is a route around Bewl Water, near Tunbridge Wells (summer only).

CHALK & CHANNEL WAY – DOVER TO FOLKESTONE

The Chalk & Channel Way is a walking and cycling path along the top of the famous White Cliffs overlooking the English Channel. On a day of good visibility, you may be able to see right across to France. Crossing the Kent Downs Area of Outstanding Natural Beauty, the trail links the harbours of Dover and Folkestone and is part of National Route 2 of the National Cycle Network that connects the towns of the south coast, going through areas of great natural beauty and historical significance.

A whole series of artworks along the trail gives you every reason to stop and admire the views. *Samphire Tower* is a 10m (33ft), oak-framed and larch-clad structure that reflects nautical architecture around the UK coastline. *Coccoliths*, inspired by the microscopic skeletons left by the millions of extinct algae forming the White Cliffs, is a collection of giant concrete forms nestled into the hillside overlooking Folkestone. *On the Crest of a Wave* is two Portland stone blocks, white like the cliffs of Dover, each one supporting the figure of a swimmer in sea-green Kirkstone slate.

ROUTE INFORMATION
National Route: 2
Start: Dover Promenade by *On the Crest of a Wave* sculpture.
Finish: Folkestone Harbour.
Distance: 8 miles (13km).
Grade: Medium. Some parts are easy but there are a couple of sections with steep hills.

Surface: Gravel paths and tarmac roads.
Hills: Steep climbs but spectacular views.

YOUNG & INEXPERIENCED CYCLISTS
Around half the route is on-road and half on traffic-free trails or cycle tracks. Families travelling from Dover may prefer to start from Samphire Hoe, accessing the main route via the Samphire Hoe cycleway and tunnel (although there is a climb) and avoid the on-road climb out of the town. From Folkestone, the scarp of the Downs at the start is long and steep and not suitable for young children.

Fulmar seek out clifftop nesting sites

Dover Castle, one of the largest in Britain

REFRESHMENTS

- Lots of choice in Dover and Folkestone.
- Light refreshments available at Samphire Hoe, along with a good picnic spot. At sea level, with a steep climb back up to the route.
- Halfway along the route, there's a cliff-top cafe with spectacular views.
- The Lighthouse Inn, Capel-le-Ferne.
- Seafood stalls and pubs at Folkestone Harbour.

THINGS TO SEE & DO

- The Chalk & Channel Way travels along the

top of the famous White Cliffs of Dover, where there are good views over the English Channel – on a clear day, you can see the coast of France. The route is punctuated by a series of artworks.

Dover:

- Dover Castle, just off the route: www.english-heritage.org.uk
- Docks and Harbour: www.dover-kent.co.uk
- Knights Templar Church: foundations of a small medieval church, traditionally the site of King John's submission to the papal legate in 1213; www.english-heritage.org.uk
- Western Heights: huge fortification begun during the Napoleonic Wars and completed in the 1860s, designed to protect Dover from French invasion; only the moat can be visited; www.english-heritage.org.uk
- Samphire Hoe Picnic Site and Visitor Centre: www.samphirehoe.com
- Battle of Britain Memorial, Capel-le-Ferne.
- Listening Ears: concrete listening devices, known as sound mirrors, built along the coast in the 1930s to detect enemy aircraft.

Folkestone:

- Sunday market by the start of the route at the harbour.
- Old High Street: this cobbled street leading up to the town centre is part of the Creative

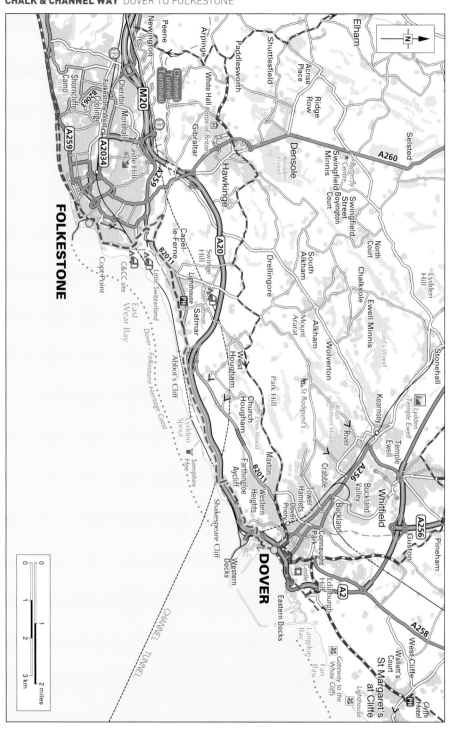

Butterfly on a viper's bugloss flower

Cycling uphill on the cliff path

'Samphire Tower' by Jony Easterby

Quarter and is lined with galleries and cafes.
- Entertainment at the Leas Cliff Hall.
- **East Cliff Sands:** the only natural sandy beach in the area. There is an adventure playground about half a mile (0.8km) to the west of Folkestone Harbour and nearby a cafe overlooking a small, man-made and sheltered sandy beach.

TRAIN STATIONS
Dover Priory; Folkestone Central.

BIKE HIRE
- **Dover White Cliff Tours:** 01303 271388; www.doverwhiteclifftours.com

FURTHER INFORMATION
- To view or print National Cycle Network routes, visit www.sustrans.org.uk
- Maps for this area are available to buy from www.sustransshop.co.uk
- **Dover Tourist Information:** 01304 205108; www.whitecliffscountry.org.uk
- **White Cliffs of Dover:** www.nationaltrust.org.uk
- **Folkestone Tourist Information:** 01303 258594; www.discoverfolkestone.co.uk

ROUTE DESCRIPTION
Start at the *On the Crest of a Wave* sculpture by Ray Smith on Waterlook Crescent by the docks in Dover. Follow Route 2 west on the traffic-free path to reach a short on-road section in Aycliff before rejoining the traffic-free path. For a good picnic place, take a detour to Samphire Hoe. Back on the route, continue on the traffic-free path with a short on-road section to Capel-le-Ferne. Follow a series of roads and traffic-free sections to Folkestone Harbour.

You can make this a circular route by going inland at Capel-le-Ferne to join Regional Route 17 (blue sign) and cycling east through West Hougham and Maxton, back to Dover.

NEARBY CYCLE ROUTES
The Chalk & Channel Way is part of National Cycle Network Route 2, which connects the towns of the south coast. To the northeast, Route 2 continues to Ramsgate and is mainly traffic-free from St Margaret's at Cliffe.To the southwest, the route, which is initially along the seafront, is flat and traffic-free most of the way to West Hythe. Part of the route travels alongside the Royal Military Canal – boats are available for hire at Hythe.

There are local cycle routes to Canterbury, but access to them is via busy roads.

PEGWELL BAY TO DOVER

The Kent coast is a beautiful place to visit by bike. This route starts at Ramsgate to the north of Pegwell Bay, one of the great English seaside towns of the 19th century. It is still famous for its sandy beaches and the start point of the ride is next to one of the largest marinas on the south coast. Pegwell Bay itself features a large nature reserve, known for its migrating waders and wildfowl, with a complete series of seashore habitats including extensive mudflats and salt marsh. A full-size replica Viking longboat rests on the low clifftops above the bay, built to commemorate the first Viking landings in England. The route continues to the historic town of Sandwich. John Montagu, 4th Earl of Sandwich, allegedly invented the snack of the same name after ordering his valet to bring him meat tucked between two pieces of bread. Along the 5-mile (8km) largely traffic-free section from Sandwich to Deal, sandy beaches and dunes give way to chalk downland and at Deal the coast of France, just 25 miles (40km) from the town, is visible on clear days. The 9-mile (14km) section from Deal to Dover runs along a stunningly scenic coastal cliff path.

ROUTE INFORMATION

Start: Ramsgate Yacht Marina.
Finish: Dover Marina.
Distance: 21 miles (33.5km).
Grade: Mostly easy with some sections on or alongside roads.
Surface: A mixture of well-surfaced tarmac and some gravel paths.
Hills: A few steady hills along the coast from Deal to Dover and a steep descent into Dover itself, but much of the route is flat.

YOUNG & INEXPERIENCED CYCLISTS

The traffic-free sections and rides along the seafront are ideal for young and inexperienced cyclists. Sections on or alongside roads seek out the quietest routes available.

REFRESHMENTS

Plenty of options in Ramsgate and Dover.
• Salutation tearoom, Sandwich.
• The Hole in the Roof, Deal.
• The Malvern, Deal.

THINGS TO SEE & DO

• Sandwich Bay Bird Observatory: nature reserves and bird observation points; 01304 617341; www.sbbot.co.uk
• Sandwich & Pegwell Bay Nature Reserve: 01622 662012; www.kentwildlifetrust.org.uk
• Sandwich Riverbus and Seal Spotting: organised seal-spotting trips on the River Stour 07958 376183; www.sandwichriverbus.blogspot.com
• Pegwell Bay Country Park: 01303 266327; www.kent.gov.uk/explorekent
• Secret Gardens, Sandwich: 01304 619 919; www.the-secretgardens.co.uk
• Deal Castle: 01304 372762; www.english-heritage.org.uk
• Deal Pier: 01304 363815; www.dealpier.com
• Dover Museum: 01304 201066; www.dover.gov.uk/museum
• Roman Painted House: said to be the finest Roman house in Britain; 01304 203279; www.dover-kent.co.uk

TRAIN STATIONS

Ramsgate; Sandwich; Deal; Walmer; Dover Priory.

BIKE HIRE

• Ken's Bikes: will collect and deliver within a 15-mile (24km) radius of Margate; 01843 221422; www.kensbikes.co.uk
• Hutchings Cycles: 01304 364945
• Deal Cycles: 01304 366080

Pegwell Bay, Ramsgate

FURTHER INFORMATION

- To view or print National Cycle Network routes, visit www.sustrans.org.uk
- Maps for this area are available to buy from www.sustransshop.co.uk
- For information on cycle routes and much more, go to www.kent.gov.uk/explorekent
- Deal and Dover Tourist Information: 01304 369576; www.whitecliffscountry.org.uk
- Ramsgate Tourist Information: 0870 2646111; www.visitthanet.co.uk
- Sandwich Tourist Information (summer): 01304 613565; www.open-sandwich.co.uk

ROUTE DESCRIPTION

With Ramsgate Yacht Marina on your left, follow signs for National Cycle Network Regional Route 15 and head south alongside Royal Parade and onto the traffic-free West Cliff and Prince Edward's Promenade. Follow signs taking you to Pegwell Road and onwards until you turn left onto the traffic-free Chalk Hill, opposite Downs Road. Join a traffic-free path along the coast alongside Sandwich Road through Cliff's End, past the Viking Ship and on to Pegwell Bay Country Park. Here you head slightly inland on the path alongside Ramsgate Road, then cross Monk's Road and follow the traffic-free Lonk's Path to avoid Great Stonar industrial works and Stonar Lake. At the end of the path turn right onto Ramsgate Road, taking care as you cross the road, for the short ride along the road into Sandwich. As you cross the bridge, turn immediately left into The Quay, following the signs for National Cycle Network Route 1. At the end of the quay car park join the traffic-free path along the river out to Sandown Road, which becomes Guildford Road and takes you past Sandwich Bay Bird Observatory. Follow the signs for NCN1 which take you south along the coast on quiet lanes past Royal Cinque Ports Golf Club as far as Deal. Turn left into Godwyn Road and right onto the marina on the seafront. Continue past the Promenade Pier and onto the Promenade, which continues south, hugging the seafront, past Walmer Castle all the way to Kingsdown. Follow local lanes through the town to Oldstairs Bay. Here you head slightly inland again on Oldstairs Road, traffic-free as far as St Margaret's at Cliffe. The route takes you left into Chapel Lane and straight across High Street into Reach Road. With the coast again visible on your left, this quiet country road follows the White Cliffs into Dover. From Upper Lane turn left into the access road for the HM Coastguard site, then right to the traffic-free path down through Langdon Cliffs, underneath the A2, along Athol Terrace and East Cliff, under the A20 and onto Marine Parade, alongside the harbour. Follow the traffic-free path alongside the harbour and sandy beaches until you reach Dover Marina.

NEARBY CYCLE ROUTES

Kent is rich in great cycle routes, including:

- The Heron Trail from Higham to Upnor on the Hoo Peninsular (Regional Route 18).
- The Coast to Cathedral (Dover to Canterbury) route following Regional Routes 16 and 17.
- The Crab and Winkle Way from Canterbury to Whitstable, following NCN1.
- Tonbridge Castle to Penshurst Place following Regional Route 12.
- Sandwich in Kent to Rye in East Sussex on NCN Routes 1 and 2.
- Ashford to Tunbridge Wells, following NCN18

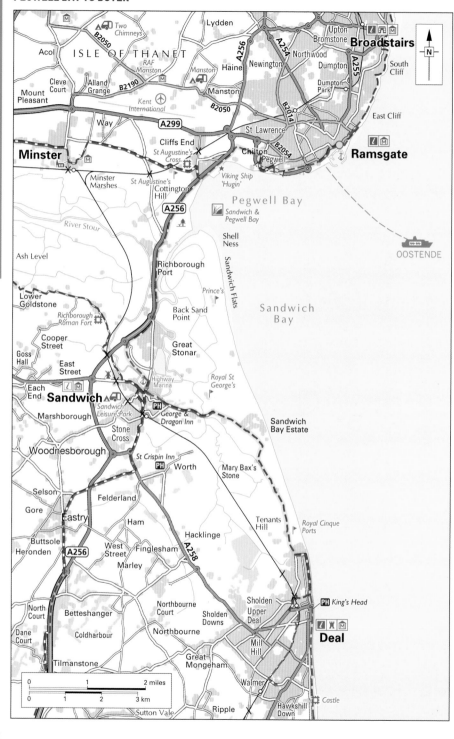

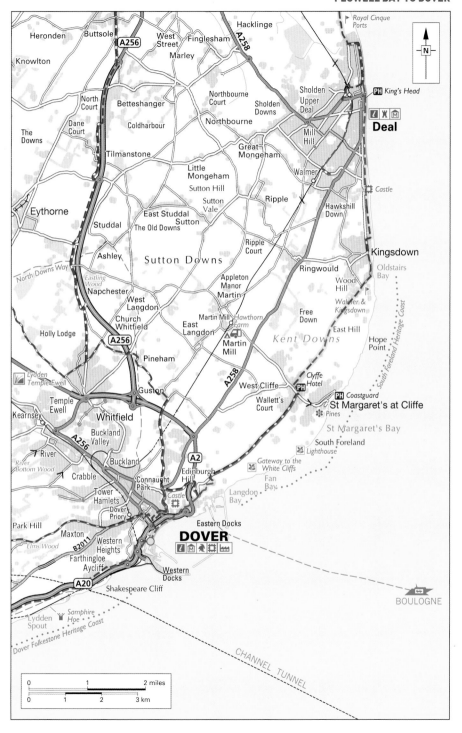

NORTH KENT COAST

This is another magnificent coastal ride. Reculver Towers are all that are left of St Mary's Church and the much earlier Roman fort, which guarded the northern entrance of the Wantsum Channel. In Roman times, this was a 2-mile (3km) wide waterway between the mainland and the Isle of Thanet, leading through to Richborough Castle, Rome's principal entry port to Britain. It eventually silted up in the 16th century, although the gravel banks at Stonar closed its southern end and isolated Sandwich from the sea centuries before.

The ride starts at Herne Bay station and approaches Reculver through the Country Park from the west. It then drops down onto the Northern Sea Wall, which was once open sea, and onto the concrete promenade that has been built all the way around the northern coast of Thanet to protect it from further erosion from the sea. It is worth choosing to cycle with the wind on your back, and if you can coincide with low tide, the sandy beaches turn this ride into a long day trip filled with numerous interludes, made all the easier by the possibility of a return trip by train.

ROUTE INFORMATION

Regional Route: 15 (Oyster Bay & Viking Coastal Trails)
Start: Herne Bay train station.
Finish: Margate train station.
Distance: 13 miles (21km). Longer option: from Herne Bay train station to Captain Digby Inn, Botany Bay (Kingsgate) 16.5 miles (26.5km).
Grade: Easy.

Surface: Concrete or tarmac promenades throughout, with reinforced grass for the one easy hill.
Hills: Mostly level promenade, with one easy hill up to Reculver Country Park.

YOUNG & INEXPERIENCED CYCLISTS

The route is particularly suitable for novices and families.

Broadstairs beach

REFRESHMENTS

- Lots of choice in Herne Bay and Margate.
- The King Ethelbert Inn, Reculver.
- Pavs Tea Gardens, Westgate-on-Sea.
- Seabell fish & chip shop, Birchington-on-Sea.

THINGS TO SEE & DO

- Powell-Cotton Museum, Quex House &

Gardens, Birchington-on-Sea: natural history dioramas; collection of cultural objects from expeditions to Africa and Asia in the late 19th century; 01843 842168; www.quexmuseum.org
- Turner Contemporary, Margate: shows of work from international artists as well as talks and lectures; 01843 233000; www.turnercontemporary.org

TRAIN STATIONS

Herne Bay; Birchington-on-Sea; Westgate-on-Sea; Margate.

BIKE HIRE

- Ken's Bikes, Margate: 01843 221422; www.kensbikes.co.uk
- The Bike Shed, Margate: 01843 228866
- Viking Coastal Trail Bike Hire, Birchington-on-Sea: 07772 037609

FURTHER INFORMATION

- To view or print National Cycle Network routes, visit www.sustrans.org.uk

HERNE BAY

Breaking waves at Botany Bay

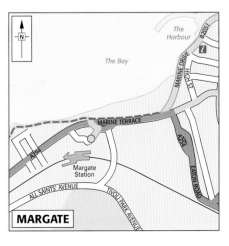

MARGATE

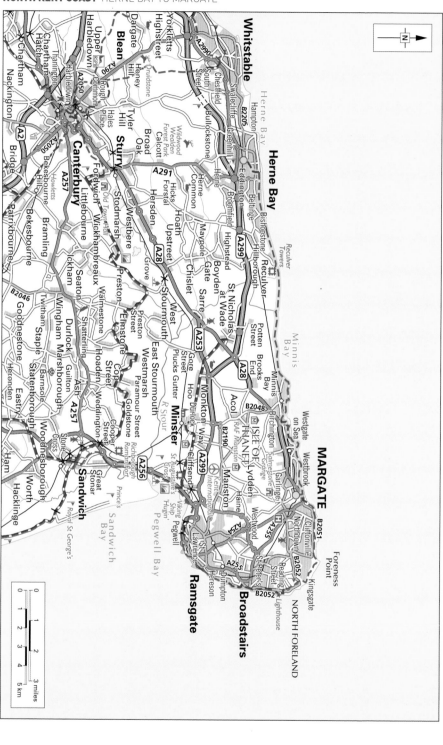

Reculver Towers, said to be haunted

- Maps for this area are available to buy from www.sustransshop.co.uk
- **Margate Tourist Information:** 0870 264 6111; visitthanet.co.uk
- **Thanet Tourist Information:** 01843 577671; www.visitthanet.co.uk

ROUTE DESCRIPTION

Leave Herne Bay station for the town centre and cross diagonally through Memorial Park to join William Street for the seafront. You are now at the eastern end of the Central Parade, with its bandstand, pier, shops and cafes. Turn right, eastwards along the seafront, and follow the East Cliff Promenade all the way to its end, where its access road climbs the hillside to the top of Hillborough Cliff. Turn left here at the start of the Oyster Bay Trail and right again to follow the path into Manor Road for the path through Reculver Country Park, which gradually slopes downhill to the towers of Reculver Church in the distance. This is a wonderful vantage point, worth dawdling over before you set out along the sea wall across the flat lands to the Isle of Thanet in the distance. Here, you join the concrete promenade/sea defence works that girdle Thanet. You are cycling at the bottom of the cliff, which can feel quite isolated when the sea is high and the

waves are thrashing against the walls. Your first real contact with the world above is at Beresford Gap for Birchington station, but, otherwise, continue on your concrete freeway until it runs out in Epple Bay at Westgate-on-Sea. Here, you follow the sea road for a little way before rejoining the Esplanade at the first opportunity, a little before Westgate Church. The Esplanade now continues, past Westgate Bay, to become the Westbrook Promenade, which leads you through to Marine Terrace opposite Margate station. There are three or four places in front of beach huts where you are asked to walk in high season. At Newgate Gap, the Viking Coastal Trail moves onto clifftop paths, still traffic-free and often very wide. They lead round to Botany Bay and the Captain Digby Inn, where the wholly traffic-free section ends. The onward route becomes a little more difficult to navigate, with sections of road round to Ramsgate and Pegwell Bay.

NEARBY CYCLE ROUTES

The 27-mile (43.5km) long Viking Coastal Trail is a circular route around the Isle of Thanet, signed just east of Reculver to St Nicholas-at-Wade and Minster for its inland section. To the south, it continues to Sandwich, where it joins National Route 1 from Canterbury to Dover.

NEXT STEPS...

We hope you have enjoyed the cycle rides in this book.

Sustrans developed the National Cycle Network to act as a catalyst for bringing cycling (and walking) back into our everyday lives. Between the 1950s and the mid-1970s cycling in the UK fell by 80%. Cycling now accounts for only about 2% of all journeys made in the UK, a fraction of what we used to achieve.

When you consider that nearly 6 in 10 car journeys are under 5 miles, it makes you wonder what the potential for increasing levels of cycling is. Evidence shows that, for local journeys under 5 miles, most of us could make 9 out of 10 journeys on foot, bike or public transport if there was more investment in making it possible to leave the car behind.

And why not? We can all be more savvy when it comes to travel. One small step becomes one giant leap if we all start walking away from less healthy lifestyles and pedalling our way towards happier children and a low carbon world.

And that's where Sustrans comes in. Sustainable travel means carbon-reducing, energy-efficient, calorie-burning, money-saving travel. Here are a few things that we think make sense. If you agree, join us.

- Snail's pace – 20mph or less on our streets where we live, go to school, shop and work – make it the norm, not just when there's snow or ice on the roads.

- Closer encounters – planning that focuses on good non-motorised access, so that we can reach more post offices, schools, shops, doctors and dentists without the car.

- People spaces – streets where kids can play hopscotch or football and be free-range, and where neighbours can meet and chat, and safe, local walking and cycling routes, to school and beyond.

- Road revolution – build miles and miles of bike paths that don't evaporate when they meet a road.

- Find our feet – campaign for pedestrian-friendly city centres, or wide boulevards with regular pedestrian crossings and slow-moving traffic.

- Better buses – used by millions, under-invested by billions and, if affordable, reliable and pleasant to use, could make local car journeys redundant.

- More car clubs – a car club on every street corner and several for every new-build estate.

- Rewards for car-sharing – get four in a car and take more than half the cars off the road.

- Trains – more of them, and cheaper.

- Become a staycationer – and holiday at home. Mountains, beaches, culture, great beer, good food and a National Cycle Network that connects them all.

If we work towards these goals we have a chance of delivering our fair share of the 80% reduction in CO_2 by mid-century that we're now committed to by law, and some of the 100% reduction that many climate experts now consider essential.

To find out more and join the movement, visit www.sustrans.org.uk